SEVEN LEAN YEARS

A Da Capo Press Reprint Series

FRANKLIN D. ROOSEVELT
AND THE ERA OF THE NEW DEAL

GENERAL EDITOR: FRANK FREIDEL
Harvard University

SEVEN LEAN YEARS

By T. J. Woofter, Jr. and Ellen Winston

DA CAPO PRESS • NEW YORK • 1972

Library of Congress Cataloging in Publication Data

Woofter, Thomas Jackson, 1893-
    Seven lean years.

    (Franklin D. Roosevelt and the era of the New Deal)
    1. U. S.—Social conditions—1933-1945.   2. Agri-
culture—Economic aspects—U. S.   3. Farm life.
4. Social problems.   5. Agriculture—U. S.
I. Winston, Ellen Engelmann (Black) 1903-   joint
author.   II. Title.   III. Series.
HD1765. 1933.W62   330.973'0916   79-39479
ISBN 0-306-70463-3

This Da Capo Press edition of *Seven Lean Years* is an
unabridged republication of the first edition published
in Chapel Hill, North Carolina, in 1939. It is
reprinted by special arrangement with the University
of North Carolina Press.

Copyright, 1939, by the University of North Carolina Press

Published by Da Capo Press, Inc.
A Subsidiary of Plenum Publishing Corporation
227 West 17th Street, New York, New York 10011

SEVEN LEAN YEARS

SEVEN
LEAN YEARS

By

T. J. WOOFTER, JR.

and

ELLEN WINSTON

CHAPEL HILL

The University of North Carolina Press

1939

MANUFACTURED IN THE UNITED STATES OF AMERICA
KINGSPORT PRESS, INC.   KINGSPORT, TENNESSEE

FOREWORD

IN THE LITERATURE of agricultural reconstruction based on the aftermath of the depression of the early thirties much has been written about the farm price structure, surplus crops, erosion, and dust storms. Not so much has been written about the human elements involved. It is the authors' conviction that the human drama of struggle, defeat, disillusion, and hunger is essentially basic and that the humanitarian has a contribution to make to rural reconstruction at least equal in importance to that of the chemist, the engineer, the agronomist, or the economist. It is, therefore, the primary objective of this book to give consideration to rural problems in terms of *human* elements as well as in terms of production, prices, and markets. The authors, through their experience in the analysis of facts relating to rural poverty, have been led inescapably to vivid realization of the seriousness of the situation. They have come to an abiding conviction that it is important to the national welfare that positive programs of agrarian and social reform be vigorously pursued in order that misery and want will not accumulate again to the same extent as in the past. At the risk of being accused of overemphasizing distress, they have, therefore, tried to make plain the causes of rural poverty and its implications in the complex pattern of our national life.

It has been the good fortune of the authors to have worked for several years in the Division of Research of the Federal Emergency Relief Administration and the Works Progress Administration, and they have thus been located on a staff primarily interested in people rather than in land or commodities. The entire rural research staffs of these agencies have contributed to the accumulation of the body of facts presented here. It was the encouragement of Harry L. Hopkins which initiated this work, and his interest in the problems treated was a stimulus to its completion. Especial acknowledgement is due to Corrington Gill, assistant administrator of the Works Progress Administration, and to Howard B. Myers, director of the Division of Social Research of the Works Progress Administration, for supervision and planning of the basic studies summarized in this book and suggestions as to the form of this work; to Carl C. Taylor, in charge of the Division of Farm Population and Rural Life of the Bureau of Agricultural Economics, Department of Agriculture; to John Fischer, director of information of the Farm Security Administration; and to Roscoe Wright and Paul Ellerbe of the Information Service, Works Progress Administration.

At the beginning of the depression the men composing the comparatively new discipline of rural sociology were ready to make their contribution to the knowledge of the elements of rural poverty. These men, on the staffs of all the principal colleges of agriculture, have labored to gain insight into the problems with which they were technically trained to deal. Most of them have contributed more or less directly to this book by the assembling of facts about rural life in their states which here have been fused into a national analysis.

The authors have tried to give a nontechnical summary of the most fundamental aspects of maladjustment in rural areas and to outline methods for the reconstruction of rural life which should prevent the recurrence of needless distress. The reader who is interested in the more voluminous technical details and in the more elaborate analyses of the topics treated in this book is referred to the research monographs of the Division of Research of the Works Progress Administration. These monographs contain the results of several years of intensive study of both urban and rural relief problems.

Various sections of the book are illustrated by cases drawn from FERA-WPA files. In every instance the name given is fictitious, but in other respects the cases are genuine.

If they have been able to illuminate any of the facts concerning destitute people in rural areas and to offer any constructive suggestions for alleviating their distress, the authors will consider that their purpose has been served.

Washington, D. C.   T. J. WOOFTER, JR.
January, 1939   ELLEN WINSTON

CONTENTS

ILLUSTRATIONS

SEVEN LEAN YEARS

CHAPTER ONE

CHANGING RURAL AMERICA

RURAL AMERICA is troubled because of sweeping changes acutely felt but only dimly understood. Persistent, searching questions are voiced whenever country life is discussed.

Is farming in America essentially different from that of twenty-five years ago? Does it still hold the promise of security which it then held? Is the frequent advocacy of the back-to-the-farm movement a wholesale solution of the ills of an all too hectic city life or can this avenue of escape benefit only a few favored individuals? What of the future of the boys and girls now growing up in farm and village homes? Has the recent distress on farms been similar to that in cities? What is the significance of the gigantic rural relief expenditures? Are we developing in the country chronically low-standard classes, more disadvantaged than the European peasant? Are some sections more favored than others? What has been the real effect of the unprecedented drought damage? Do we have depressed areas as ominous as those of the English coal mines? What are the handicaps under which rural institutions operate in the effort to provide the necessary services to people in the open country? Are there means of bringing back to rural dwellers some of the richer values of life and of increasing their security to the point of guarantees against the recurrence of future distress as intense and widespread as that of recent years? What is the part which the federal government should play in mapping policies bearing on these problems?

These are the questions to which the following chapters are addressed. They are an effort to take a sober look at the facts which are all too often beclouded with sentimentalism or political claptrap, neither of which can be expected to contribute greatly to the rational reconstruction of rural life.

The need for rural relief during the early nineteen-thirties was without precedent. This is the starting point toward the understanding of a faltering agricultural system, of decadent rural industries, and of rural families far less favored than city families in the struggle for comfort and security. The cry for public assistance was one of the most tangible, measurable manifestations of the dislocation of rural life. With this in mind it becomes important to see why this depression was different and more severe in its effects on rural areas than were the depressions of the past, to realize that a creeping blight was sapping the vitality of American agriculture before 1929, operating gradually but accumulating its effects until the financial collapse impressed the situation on the public. These deep currents slowly undermining the physical and economic foundations of agriculture were: the more rapid rise in the prices of things which the farmer bought than in the prices of things which he sold, mounting debt, loss of markets, shrinking wage opportunities in mines and forests, soil depletion and erosion, and concentration on money crops. The substitution of machines for men also limited employment.

This book treats these physical and economic handicaps of agriculture, but it is primarily interested in the resulting human problems. It analyzes the dilemma arising because the increase of the nation's population is coming largely from farms. Even in normal times agricultural opportunity does not expand rapidly enough to afford sufficient employment for the new generations, compelling a large proportion of the young people to leave the home community for the city when they are ready to work. Even this alternative of migration was cut off by the depression and for that reason perplexed farm youth had no place to go to get a start. Consequently, many of them "took to the road," and many more stayed as unneeded and unpaid workers in the parental household. This rural picture also portrays the growth of the landless classes in American agriculture, the laborers and croppers whose share in the income is meager and whose lack of economic security is disheartening. It points out that the farm population, with only one dollar in ten of the nation's income, is charged with rearing and educating one out of three of the nation's children and thus makes a heavy financial contribution to the industrial sections while straining the rural taxpaying ability to support the necessary educational, public health, and public welfare services. In addition, it is noteworthy that these fundamental causes of distress multiply in some particularly unfortunate sections and are reinforced by natural calamities, such as drought, producing widespread problem areas— regions of weakness in the nation's economic and social fabric.

This is the situation out of which arose the need for public aid to alleviate human distress. Work relief projects have contributed to the permanent assets of rural communities through the conservation of forests, soil, and water and through the improvement of health and educational facilities, but, as far as the individuals on relief are concerned, public assistance is manifestly a palliative—a temporary necessity to alleviate suffering but not a preventive of future distress. The first need is a fundamental program of rehabilitation of individuals through relocation and loans designed to put them on their feet, and through instruction and community services to keep them on their feet. But the individual alone is powerless in many situations. Even more necessary than individual aid as a preventive of future recurrence of disorganization is the replanning of an American agriculture and community life which will yield its workers a fair return and a reasonable protection from the insecurity which arises from exposure to the risks of a complex industrial system.

The improvement of rural life has been continuously agitated for many years. Country life commissions date back to the administration of Theodore Roosevelt, and farm aid has been the subject of countless investigations and organizations. Throughout this process the activities of the federal government in behalf of the farmer have increased, taking the form first of educational and advisory aid, then of the development of magnificent scientific bureaus and the extension service of the Department of Agriculture. It required the drama of the depression, however, to focus the attention of the nation upon some of the more human elements in the situation.

NATION-WIDE SIGNIFICANCE

Agriculture supports more people than any other single major employment group although it has declined since 1870 from the position of employing over half of the nation's workers to that of employing less than one fourth.

It still supports ten times as many as mining, four times as many as building, three times as many as iron and steel, and over twice as many as transportation. Moreover, the fortunes of a large part of the village trades and services are determined by farm prosperity or decline.

The well-being of over a quarter of the nation is bound up with the fortunes of the tillers of the soil; and, to the extent to which manufacturers depend on them as customers, the prosperity of industry is conditioned by the purchasing power of the farmer and of the agricultural villager.

The problems of agriculture are not confined to any one section of the nation. Although the character of these problems varies from region to region, the farmer is a substantial element in the regional life of every section except the metropolitan areas of the North Atlantic Seaboard. Thus, the maladjustments of agriculture are nation-wide in their effects and should be the concern of all people.

LONG-TIME TRENDS

American agriculture has changed radically through the decades, the changes moving across the country from east to west. The pioneer stage survived in isolated regions as long as there was free land. Behind the pioneers came the money crop exploiters in those sections particularly adapted to cotton, tobacco, wheat, corn, cattle, or truck. These have gone through a cycle in which quick, high profits, drained from a virgin soil, have been followed by a smaller margin of profit on acres whose fertility has been lowered or whose topsoil has been allowed to wash away. The nation, therefore, faces a new phase of conservation and more intensive use of the improvable lands.

To the extent that human maladjustment is the result of

these changes it is apparent that the present situation of the farmer is largely the result of long-time processes. As will become clear in the following chapters, the economic maladjustments began to make themselves felt markedly just after the World War, and the depression in agriculture preceded the depression in industry by several years. The seven leanest years, however, were the period from 1931 through 1937, when the effects of industrial collapse were piled upon the effects of agricultural disadvantage.

It was in this period that the accumulating difficulties came to a head—when the unemployed in cities added to the burdened rural population by moving back, when overproduction and shrinking markets piled up huge surpluses, when wages which had supplemented farm incomes dried up, when large-scale public relief was extended in rural areas for the first time, and when agitation for farm aid mounted to a national crescendo and the government began gropingly to seek the solutions of farm problems.

PREVENTION VS. ALLEVIATION OF DISTRESS

No thinking American wants relief loads to pile up again. With the return of prosperity, however, the public is likely to forget once more the man who exists so near the margin of want, especially the rural dweller who may be out of sight and out of mind, since the most distressed rural sections are off the beaten paths. The policy makers may condone conditions as "natural" which if unchecked will again mean human misery as well as a staggering relief bill when the economic weather once more grows stormy.

A long step toward prevention was taken with the initiation of the unemployment insurance program but, as constituted at present, this program does not go far enough. It does not cover agricultural workers nor a large propor-

A Large Relief Family on Poor Land

FSA, USDA

Under the Sky's Shelter

tion of workers in rural nonagricultural industries. Likewise, the recent wages and hours legislation fails to cover many classes of rural workers. Aid to the aged, aid to the blind, and aid to dependent children, although expanding rapidly under the Social Security Program, is still inadequate in many states, both in amounts granted and cases covered. Health insurance is yet to come. The most fundamental measures of prevention concern the readjustment of the balance between agriculture and industry, the readjustment of population to land, and the preservation of the nation's greatest assets in its water, forests, and soil. In the field of public welfare it can be clearly demonstrated that "an ounce of prevention is worth a pound of cure."

For the genuine humanitarians who grasp the tragedy of these seven lean years the slogan should be, "It must not happen again." What the nation needs is an attitude toward unemployment and dependency similar to, and as sound in its common sense as, the ideas underlying hygienic medicine, which is constantly vigilant in the application of preventive measures rather than waiting to fight epidemics after they develop.

CHAPTER TWO

THE SIGNIFICANCE OF RURAL

DISTRESS

THE FINANCIAL memory of the American public is notoriously short. When the stock market rises, past hard times are forgotten and future possibilities of hard times ignored. Although the market has made several excursions in both directions since 1929, it is possible for some to remember the accumulated distress of the first hard years of depression.

EARLY DEPRESSION CONDITIONS

It is not difficult to imagine ourselves back in the summer of 1933 in a formerly bustling small city set in a land of once thriving farms. Prosperity had brought increase to the city of seventy thousand people in twenty years. Most of this increase had been supplied by the movement of ambitious young people from near-by farms, a movement which, on a national scale, was building all cities.

But in 1933 the movement from farms was different. Passing through the city were hundreds of jobless, homeless, hungry wanderers. Through back alleys went constant files of able-bodied men rummaging for scraps in garbage cans.   Lines of freight cars passed, each train topped with a frieze of sooty "free passengers."   These freight riders were so numerous that trainmen tacitly ignored their presence, and let them ride.   Equally numerous, and more likely to come to the attention of the average citizen, were the hitchhikers who followed the main highways in hopeful anticipation of a lift.   In those days, and regardless of modes of travel, they were all looked on as "hoboes" or "bums."   Few knew why the number of hoboes had increased tenfold.   They were not the traditional type of tramp but depression jetsam, many of them having left impoverished homes in a desperate effort to seek their own salvation.   Many were tragically young and for that reason were honestly hopeful of finding something better beyond the horizon.   Others were disheartened and disillusioned. Most of them had little skill to offer in the labor market, even if work had been available.   They were unskilled or semiskilled or were fresh from the farm.   Some had yet to find their first jobs.   Many were desperately eager for any job by which they could earn even a meal.

Such an army of drifters, unattached, constantly on the move, had its sinister social significance.   Its members were the surface symptoms of a relatively new phenomenon— mass rural distress.   They were, however, merely the symptoms, for back of each wanderer there were hundreds who suffered at home.

Large-scale public dependence of rural dwellers had been previously unknown.   A few old and incapacitated people were always to be found in almshouses or "on the county," but in past hard times farmers or villagers who were down on their luck were expected to live on their neighbors, their relatives, or their credit, or simply tighten their belts until better times arrived.   Moreover, until comparatively recent years there were fertile lands in the West to which they still might migrate.

In periods of economic distress it was assumed that private charity would take up the task of caring for the urban unemployed; but not for those in the country. Bread lines, soup kitchens, and flophouses, familiar enough in the city, were unknown in the open country. In the depression of the early thirties a few associated charities extended their benefits beyond the limits of cities, but most of these were forced to restrict or actually to cease their aid early in 1932 and 1933 when the sources of their funds were frozen in closed banks and panicky pocketbooks.

Many of the jobless wanderers in the early days of the depression were immediately or recently from rural localities. Millions of them had poured into the cities from the farms during the decade from 1920 to 1930. When adversity came, those who had most recently migrated from farms and small towns were often the first to be cast adrift in accordance with the "last hired, first fired" policy prevalent in industry. Urban relief loads were higher than rural loads, partly because they included many from the country. There is, therefore, no way of measuring accurately the rural incidence of the depression relief load.

HEAVY RELIEF LOADS

In spite of the disheartening conditions of 1933 we were assured that prosperity was on the way. It is plain enough in retrospect that, though the economic indices of prosperity began their painful climb when the trough of the depression was reached some time in 1932, the relief rolls continued to mount. For many months after the autumn of 1929 the nation saw unemployment increase rapidly without making any effective counterattack. At the time when "prosperity" began its return, there were an estimated fifteen million unemployed, many of whom had been jobless for as long as three years.

This unemployment estimate, moreover, did not include the unemployed or underemployed farmers and home farm laborers. If they lived on farms they were regarded as "employed," no matter how little income their efforts produced. Eventually, many of the unprofitably employed workers, as well as many unemployed, were compelled to seek public assistance. The burden first overwhelmed private charity and then swamped state and local organizations. It proved too large for the resources placed at the disposal of the states by the Reconstruction Finance Corporation. The accumulation of distress was so great that relief rolls continued to mount for almost two years after the first federal emergency relief was granted in May, 1933.

By January, 1935, the total number of households receiving general relief from the federal government, households in which members were receiving old age or blind pensions or mothers' assistance, wages from the Civilian Conservation Corps, transient relief, and teachers' salaries under the emergency education program, farm families which were receiving rural rehabilitation loans, and households receiving aid from private agencies was nearly six and a half million. This means that in a single month between twenty and twenty-five million persons, or roughly one out of every five persons in the United States, were the recipients of public or private assistance. While it is not possible to determine the urban-rural division of all types of relief, it seems safe to say that approximately two and a half million rural families containing more than ten million persons were receiving help at that time.

These figures, stupendous though they are, tell only part of the story. Families were constantly coming on and going off relief rolls. Although many were able to regain self-support and leave the relief rolls more or less permanently, thousands of rural families had not yet sought public assistance in January, 1935, but applied later. Because of this type of turnover, it seems conservative to say that about three and a half million rural households, more than one out of every four, received public or private assistance for a longer or shorter period during the great depression and its aftermath. If to these three and a half million rural households at one time or another on relief there are added the hundreds of thousands of others which were near the borderline but were able to stretch meager private resources through the depression or to "double up" with relatives, it appears that as far as rural families are concerned it is entirely too conservative to estimate that only one third of the people are ill-fed, ill-housed, and ill-clad.

The trend in the number of rural households on relief from 1931 through 1934 mounted more sharply than the urban increase. Estimates indicate that from a high in January, 1935, of about two and a half million, rural families aided by all public assistance programs declined steadily until the summer of 1936.

The ravages of the 1936 drought again caused rural distress to mount in the Plains States sufficiently to offset the declines elsewhere, and programs were expanded to carry drought-stricken families through the winter. With the new planting season of 1937 and improved employment conditions in private industry, rural relief and wage assistance rolls again started downward and the decline was fairly steady until the latter months of 1937. Then the interruption of the upswing in industry, low prices for agricultural commodities, normal seasonal unemployment, and localized drought again piled up rural distress in some sections.

A recent report from the Arkansas Delta, which is typical of conditions in numerous southern counties, indicates the serious situation which faced many rural families as late as January, 1939. It had been estimated in the preceding January that there were between a thousand and fifteen hundred needy unemployed families in a single Delta county and that three hundred of them were penniless. Their almost equal division between farm and nonfarm reflected an acute situation in all types of rural employment, and later reports indicated little change after a year.

This county is in one of the most fertile areas in the world. It had had no drought or floods. Its troubles were wholly man-made. It had just produced a record cotton crop but the prices were so low that tenants did not make enough to carry them through the winter. Disorganization of rural industries was partly responsible. Uncertainty of large landlords as to their prospective quotas under a new crop control act added to the general instability, while increasing substitution of tractors for man power points to added unemployment of tenants and laborers in the future.

DIVERSE NEEDS

As in any large group of people there was a wide diversity of characteristics in the relief population. It included people of all degrees of employability from the totally incompetent to the fully employable. Furthermore, there were varying shades of actual employment from the totally unemployed to those fully employed but earning too little to meet the needs of a large family. The group included normal families as well as the widowed and or-

phaned. It included part-time farmers, full-time farmers
failing to make a go of farming, displaced tenants, unemployed farm laborers, and casual, partially employed laborers. In addition there were village workers who had
little relation to agriculture.

Because of the great diversity of occupations and the
intermediate position which they occupy between the
farm and city populations, rural-industrial workers have not
received proportionate attention. Yet they included well
over one sixth of all gainful workers in 1930 and supported
about one fifth of the total population. On the one hand,
they felt the pressure of agricultural maladjustments because the fortunes of a large part of the village population
are determined by farm prosperity or decline. On the
other hand, industrial villages felt the effects of urban unemployment and of the decline of such typically rural
industries as lumbering and mining. Thus in many instances conditions arising out of the depression of the early
thirties reached their height among the rural nonagricultural
workers, and today few national problems are more compelling than that of stranded villages.

To meet the needs of so diverse a group was a complex
task. The family case-work methods evolved in cities did
not always fit the rural family and new techniques had to
be worked out. The variety of the types of people in need
meant that varied kinds of relief had to be administered.
Their needs ranged from temporary, slight assistance of a
few dollars to tide them over an emergency to full institutional care. Some of the needy required food, some fuel,
some clothing, some medical care, some a cow or a horse
or garden supplies, and some merely needed advice and instruction. Their needs covered the full range of the basic
human necessities.

STAGGERING COSTS

The total relief bill for the tremendous burden of urban and rural destitution has been staggering, costing public treasuries and private donors more than thirteen billion dollars between January, 1931, and December, 1937. Relief grants made to rural areas accounted for a larger and larger proportion of the total up to the peak in January, 1935, and then for an increasingly smaller proportion through 1936 with a leveling off in 1937.

Out of the seven-year relief bill of over thirteen billion dollars, the rural cost was over three and one-half billion dollars. The rural expenditures were less than the urban, both because of the smaller number of cases and because of the smaller grants to rural than to urban cases. The figures take no account of special loans and benefits for agriculture, which operated both to help keep farm families off relief and to reduce the needs of those who were forced to apply for public assistance.

To think of the problem only in terms of millions of relief cases and billions of dollars is not enough, however. To come to the full realization of what widespread destitution means, one must think in terms of human waste, disappointment, discouragement, breaking of family ties, defeated young men and women, disabling illness, undernourished children, and actual cold and hunger. For millions of men, women, and children caught in the meshes of the depression through no fault of their own, there was literally no way out through their unaided efforts. In the face of complex economic circumstances, individuals found themselves helpless. And the expenditures of the federal government, tremendous as they were, were only sufficient to provide the bare necessities of life.

Those who have long enough memories to recall the despair of millions in 1932 and early 1933 realize that if some such expenditures had not been made, the life, security, and self-respect of a great segment of the population would have been even more seriously jeopardized. Instead of a payable financial debt, the nation would rapidly have stored up malnutrition, disease, crime, and defeatism.

Huge sums have been spent to ameliorate the effects of recent depression. Many citizens are aghast at the thought of the great expenditures which may again be necessary if there should be a recurrence of such drought and depression needs in rural areas as were characteristic of the early nineteen-thirties. Such expenditures as have been made were the only alternative to callous neglect of suffering. But the application of palliatives in the future, after distress had been allowed to accumulate, would be thoroughly uneconomic and, while it must be condoned for the past, can never again be acceptable as a method of even temporary solution of widespread rural problems.

Before anyone can plan wisely for prevention, it is important that the basic causes of rural distress be understood. As these causes are described in succeeding pages, it will become evident that they arise from essentially preventable situations, physical and social and economic conditions which can be improved, not with great rapidity but consistently over a long period as the result of constructive planning and patient achievement. The intensity and unprecedented volume of the recent distress are convincing evidence of the pressing need for such planning.

CHAPTER THREE

INSECURITY IN AGRICULTURE

WHY DID masses of farmers need government assistance during the past depression when they had managed to pull through previous depressions without asking for help? Why should farmers as a class need help since they supposedly obtain subsistence from the land on which they live?

The answers to these questions are to be found in trends which have been operating for a long time, some of which date back to the previous century. They were insidiously undermining the security of the farmer, and the foundations of American agriculture thus weakened were vulnerable to the onslaught of the depression. These long-time corrosive elements which underlie farm distress are: adverse farm prices, years of soil abuse, of allowing water to leach away the precious topsoil, of putting all the eggs into a one-crop basket, of cultivation of wide areas which should have been left in native grasses or forest, of accumulating debts, and of exhaustion of supplementary forest and mineral resources. These blighting forces had persistently undermined the economic foundation of American farming and the security of American farmers. But such long-range economic factors account for only part of the recent agrarian difficulties. Depression factors began to operate and distress on farms was intensified when markets and financial institutions became disorganized. Burdened with accumulated debts, their savings exhausted or lost through bank failures, and unable to secure credit, hundreds of thousands of farmers throughout the United States were forced off the land and onto public assistance rolls, while others remaining on the land were unable to feed their families.

Some of the long-time factors in agriculture that have played a significant role in the destitute circumstances of thousands of families during recent years are well illustrated by the experiences of John Henderson,* life-long farmer in the Great Plains. Henderson started as a farm owner in 1904, paying $3,000 down on his two-hundred-forty-acre farm with the balance of $6,600 carried by a bank mortgage. All of the acreage was placed under cultivation in succeeding years except twenty-five acres in pasture and four acres in woodland. The farm livestock was adequate—five horses, twelve cows, twelve sheep, a flock of chickens, etc. Over the years the mortgage was not wiped out and Henderson had a struggle with interest and taxes. In 1928 when chattel mortgages likewise became pressing, foreclosure followed. A few unsuccessful years as a tenant on a submarginal farm of one hundred and twenty acres followed and in the fall of 1933 relief became necessary.

It may seem that this was a case wherein neither depression nor drought was a basic trouble. However, agricultural depression was felt in the Northwest long before industrial depression arose in the East. Many farmers put their savings into a piece of land, got along moderately well

---

* All names in case histories are fictitious.

until the World War period, then spent a little lavishly, often overexpanding, and were wiped out about the time that Henderson lost his holdings.

ADVERSE PRICES

For more than a century after 1800 there was a general upward trend in agricultural prices in relation to those of industry. After 1920, however, the prices received by farmers began to decline in relation to retail prices of goods which they had to buy. From then until 1932 the general trend was downward except for a few good years during the middle nineteen-twenties. Even in the relatively good years between 1923 and 1929, farm income failed to increase as rapidly as total national income.[1] The decreased farm income was not momentous at first, but, when it continued over a long period, the disparity in prices received by farmers and prices which they had to pay steadily drained their resources. Between 1929 and 1933 prices paid to farmers declined two thirds while prices they had to pay to farm and to live declined only one third.[2] In 1909 almost 35 per cent of the gainfully occupied were dependent on agriculture and received 19 per cent of the national income, while in 1930 the 21 per cent of the gainfully occupied dependent on agriculture received only about 9 per cent of the income.[3] Thus, the proportion of the income going to agriculture had decreased much more rapidly than the proportion of the population in agriculture.

---

[1] Mordecai Ezekiel and Louis H. Bean, *Economic Bases for the Agricultural Adjustment Act* (U. S. Dept. of Agriculture, Washington, December, 1933), p. 6.

[2] U. S. Dept. of Agriculture, Bureau of Agricultural Economics.

[3] Louis H. Bean, "Increasing the Farmers' Share of the National Income," in *The Agricultural Situation* (U. S. Dept. of Agriculture, Bureau of Agricultural Economics, Washington, Feb. 1, 1935), pp. 2–9.

Rumblings of agrarian discontent were heard all during the nineteen-twenties and early nineteen-thirties. During this period there was a recurrence of the farm uprisings which had occurred during the granger movement of the eighteen-seventies and the farm alliance days of the late eighteen-eighties and early eighteen-nineties. Farm holidays, milk strikes, interference with mortgage sales, and incessant demands on the federal government for "farm relief" were visible manifestations of unrest. These for the most part were not taken seriously by the general public, being dismissed by many as a new brand of radicalism.

In 1930–31, in an effort to stabilize prices, the federal government bought some of the excess wheat and cotton, but this action was inadequate and relatively unsuccessful. During the period of falling prices the production of export crops remained geared to World War conditions and farm surpluses gradually mounted. The final push necessary to demoralize a weak price structure came from the drastic reductions in United States exports to foreign markets, following the recovery of European agriculture and the development of new agricultural areas in other countries, and from shrinking domestic purchasing power.

COMMERCIALIZATION AND DEBT

The disorganization of farm credit and of farm markets followed a change in the agricultural system that contributed increasingly to growing insecurity. Less and less of the family living was produced on the farm. More and more acreage was devoted to cash crop production, particularly in areas specializing in cotton, tobacco, corn, or wheat, although other specialty crops were cultivated with equal intensity in smaller areas. The cotton plantation of the nineteen-twenties was less self-sustaining than the slave plantation of the eighteen-sixties. The newly emerging farm economics was one predominantly of cash crops and markets, pushing the farmer more and more into a position similar to that of the industrialist in that he was left vulnerable to losses of markets and to financial crises. And the position of the hired farm laborer became like that of the industrial laborer, who is subject to layoff in hard times. When the financial collapse came, it was not cushioned by home production of a large share of the goods needed by the farm family, and operator and laborer alike lacked money with which to purchase their basic needs.

Along with the change in farming habits came a change in buying habits. Like his city brother, the farmer bought automobiles, radios, and washing machines on the installment plan. In addition he sometimes invested heavily in large-scale machinery with which to cultivate his expanding acreage. With the price differential against him his sales did not always pay for these purchases, and he ate into his capital by mortgaging the farm. Accordingly, the farm mortgage debt increased from three and one-third billion dollars in 1910 to nine and one-half billion dollars in 1928, in spite of the diminishing relative value of agricultural products and in spite of the fact that land values per acre in 1928 were not greatly above the 1910 level.[4] This expanded indebtedness measures the extent to which the farmer was living off his capital. Sons of men who formerly shuddered at the word "mortgage" could not withstand the temptation of relatively easy credit and adopted this means of securing cash.

One of the earliest symptoms of depression distress in rural areas was the frequent foreclosures, and one of the

---

[4] David L. Wickens, *Farm-Mortgage Credit*, Technical Bulletin No. 288 (U. S. Dept. of Agriculture, Washington, February, 1932).

large groups which appeared later on the relief rolls consisted of farm owners who had lost their land under foreclosure and tenants who had been turned adrift when landlords lost their farms to banks or corporations that were
not in a position to supply credit to tenants. In fact, much
of the "displacement" of tenants which has been attributed
to the Agricultural Adjustment Administration was in reality attributable to early depression foreclosures, voluntary
acreage reduction, and mechanization. The relief rolls of
the cotton states cared for far more tenants in 1933 and
1934 than in 1935 after the effects of the AAA were fully
operative.

Associated with the top-heavy farm debt structure were
the high and ever mounting tax rates. In some cases
farmers' tax assessments amounted to as much as one third
of their net income.[5] With high taxes and declining gross
incomes, tax delinquencies inevitably increased. County
records of tax collections show that 85 per cent or more
of the land was tax delinquent in some parts of the drought
area. Often the farmers' taxes were delinquent year after
year [6] as hard times increased the financial burdens they had
shouldered under the impetus of expanding markets and
increased production.

LOSS OF OUTSIDE INCOME

One of the large agricultural classes whose straits were
revealed by the depression consisted of farmers who had

---

[5] P. G. Beck and M. C. Forster, *Six Rural Problem Areas, Relief-
Resources-Rehabilitation*, Research Monograph 1, Federal Emergency Relief Administration, Division of Research, Statistics, and Finance (Washington, 1935), p. 14.

[6] R. S. Kifer and H. L. Stewart, *Farming Hazards in the Drought Area*,
Research Monograph xvi, Works Progress Administration, Division of
Social Research (Washington, 1938), Chap. 1.

never made their entire living from the farm. For them farming was largely a side line, and nearly all cash income was derived from other employment. According to a rough estimate about one third of the rural families combine to some extent industrial activity with farming. If these part-time farmers were so fortunate as to be located near relatively continuous opportunities for industrial employment or even partial employment, their position was not too serious, but if their only industrial opportunity was in some small plant which could not weather the depression, if they were located in an area of exhausted natural resources, such as the Appalachian Mountains or the cut-over area around the Great Lakes, the loss of supplementary employment was disastrous. The collapse of many small rural manufacturing plants and of mining and lumbering, together with the shrinkage of employment on public roads and on miscellaneous rural and small-town construction, further restricted the earning power of part-time farmers.

There was a dogged attempt near unprofitable mines and logged-off hillsides to obtain sustenance from the soil. Through the coal valleys of the Appalachians the discouraged miners have moved up the slopes to struggle with land never intended for the plow.

Without sufficient good land to provide even a meager living for their families, and unsuited both by temperament and experience for full-time agricultural labor, this group of part-time farmers early came on relief. In spite of optimistic theories as to the value of a small farming enterprise in times of economic crisis, a necessary minimum of industrial employment is found to be basic to its success.[7]

---

[7] R. H. Allen, L. S. Cottrell, Jr., W. W. Troxell, Harriet L. Herring, and A. D. Edwards, *Part-Time Farming in the Southeast*, Research Monograph IX, Works Progress Administration, Division of Social Research (Washington, 1937), p. xxxiv.

These relationships of industrial-agricultural employment as well as the fluctuation in demand for agricultural products emphasize the interdependence of farm and city. In addition, thousands of families in agricultural villages prosper or fail as the surrounding farmers prosper or fail. The conditions affecting these villagers and those dependent on scattered rural industry are given special treatment in Chapter IX.

SMALL FARMS

In areas of rapid population increase, where the supply of good land is limited, the subdivision of acreage has often reduced the size of farms below the minimum necessary to produce subsistence on that type of land. This problem of lack of sufficient land is often a factor in part-time farming. In periods when nonagricultural employment is normal, the small size of the farm is not a handicap. In many isolated sections, however, families are attempting to wrest a living from small acreages which will not produce sufficient quantities of foodstuffs to supply their needs. The number of these small acreages is mounting. Between 1930 and 1935 farms of less than twenty acres in size increased by more than 36 per cent.[8]

In the cut-over areas of northern Michigan, Wisconsin, and Minnesota, most of the land was formerly covered with virgin forest, but the timber resources are now almost exhausted. Many families settling in this area depended on part-time work in the lumbering industry for their cash income, and when this failed they had only marginal farm land to fall back on. Families living in the open country of this section often have farms of forty, sixty, and eighty

---

[8] *United States Census of Agriculture: 1935.*

Losing Soil

WPA

Substitutes for Man Power

acres, with sometimes less than ten acres cleared.[9] Since this is poor land, an adequate livelihood from agriculture is virtually impossible.

Countless farms in all areas of the Great Plains are not large enough to yield sufficient income to meet the carrying charges on the land and other operating expenses and to provide a decent living for the farm family. In a typical North Dakota county there are many farms of less than 280 acres which have only a little over 100 acres of cropland and about 50 acres of pasture, which in that area obviously will provide for only a small number of livestock.[10] If the entire crop acreage of these farms were planted to wheat, the most profitable crop in the area, the average value of the crop on the basis of the usual yield and at the 1930–34 farm price would be $558 on farms with 114 acres of cropland and $1,175 on farms with 240 acres. This area, incidentally, offers little nonagricultural employment to supplement farmers' incomes.

All surveys of the characteristics of rural relief households have shown that the farmers who have needed assistance have operated acreages smaller than the average for their respective areas. Lacking enough land in terms of farming practices in their communities, or having insufficient acreages of low productivity, they were inevitably marked as among the first who would succumb to agricultural distress.

SUBMARGINAL LAND

The problems of land use in farming on submarginal land have three related causes: misuse of land, soil exhaustion, and soil erosion.

---

[9] Beck and Forster, *op. cit.,* pp. 11–15.
[10] Kifer and Stewart, *op. cit.,* Chap. 1.

Much of the soil misuse in the Great Plains has resulted from a mistaken substitution of field crops for grazing on land which afforded good pasturage but which eventually proved unsuited to grain production. Unwise land use in large areas has usually accompanied mass movements that were encouraged by speculators and sometimes by the government itself. The government, under steady political pressure, early adopted a homestead policy in the West which substituted tilled crops for grazing under conditions of extremely doubtful wisdom in some sections. Settlers poured westward to continue the farming methods suitable to the more humid climate from which they came. Only as they adopted dry-farming methods and as acreages were gradually expanded did they arrive at a satisfactory equilibrium between natural factors and agricultural techniques. Adoption of such practices, however, and the increased demand for wheat resulting from the World War led them to overturn increasingly large expanses of virgin sod. Native grasses no longer anchored the soil. In a county in the Texas Panhandle where an extensive program for repairing the damage due to soil erosion has now been undertaken, a group of selected farmers reported in the summer of 1935 that from one third to one half of their cropland had been seriously damaged by wind erosion and drought and that in addition almost one half had been slightly damaged.[11]

Another type of land misuse which is widespread throughout the cut-over region around the Great Lakes and in the South is the result of the exploitation of forest resources. Timber companies, when they have stripped off the forests, seek further profits by selling the cleared land for farming. In the West land companies and railways

[11] *Ibid.*, Chap. III.

have promoted occupation without regard to the permanent success of the settlers.

One-crop agriculture, unwise systems of rotation, and failure to restore topsoil have practically destroyed the natural wealth of many areas. To offset this loss farmers have been increasingly compelled to use expensive fertilizer. Some farmers with land of a gross productivity rarely above twenty dollars per acre must spend nearly one third of that for fertilizer to obtain even a low return. Fertilizer costs are heavier in the South than elsewhere; almost three fifths of the nation's fertilizer bill is paid by twelve southeastern states.[12] The farmers' national expenditure for fertilizer in 1929 was more than two hundred and seventy-one million dollars. One third of this was for cotton farms, and another third was for crop specialty, fruit, and truck farms.[13]

When soil becomes exhausted, there are three alternatives: heavy expenditures for fertilizer, the long and tedious process of restoring the soil's fertility, or abandonment. In many rural sections vast acreages once under cultivation have been left to revert to natural vegetative covering.

Rain, the farmers' best friend when the soil needs moisture, is their worst enemy when methods of clean cultivation have exposed the land to the effects of running water. Attrition of the elements has stripped the topsoil from great slopes and continues its ravages. Deeply gullied fields and muddy rivers bear witness to our waste of agriculture's prime resource. That ever more and more acres might go under the plow, trees and grass cover, the natural preservers and builders of topsoil, have been ruthlessly removed, exposing new fields to destruction. In some sections only

---

[12] *Fifteenth Census of the United States: 1930*, Agriculture Vol. II, Part 1.

[13] *Ibid.*

the barren subsoil remains and farming in these clay beds is both unproductive and expensive.

Dr. Carl Sauer, the geographer, has described his pilgrimages to the homes of some of the great men of a century ago. In many instances he noted that they were located on land which is now gullied and bare of topsoil, witnessing the attrition of nature which has changed them from the once productive homesteads of prosperous families to national shrines set in barren lands.

According to a recent report of the National Resources Board, unwise agricultural practices have resulted in the complete loss for farming purposes of thirty-five million acres. The topsoil has been entirely or almost entirely removed from between three and four times that acreage, and another one hundred million acres is showing increasing signs of deterioration.[14]

Thus, ill-considered land use has been a major factor in the extensive agricultural problems of recent years. Yet this is a field in which preventive and remedial measures are both relatively simple and relatively sure. Where destruction has made attempts at restoration impractical, guided migration to more fertile areas appears to be the wisest solution.

MECHANIZATION

The increasing use of machinery in crop production not only reduces the need for man power but also increases the insecurity of the jobs of those who do not have capital. Wheat, corn, and latterly cotton have required less and less man power as the use of tractors and harvesting machinery has expanded.

---

[14] *National Resources Board Report, December 1, 1934,* Part i, Sec. i, p. 17.

Increases in agricultural efficiency have caused a steady increase in output per man. It has been estimated that the average worker on farms produced two and one half times as much in 1930 as in 1870.[15] In other words, had the demand for agricultural products been no greater in 1930 than it was in 1870, these products could have been grown with two fifths of the labor supply. It is estimated, for instance,[16] that since the period 1909–13 there has been a reduction of two hundred and forty million man-hours in the annual use of labor for wheat production and of one hundred and forty-three million man-hours for the production of oats. The production of cotton, slow to be mechanized in the past, shows tendencies in the late nineteen-thirties of rapid change in some areas, owing to the introduction of the tractor and the cotton chopper. As a result of the continuously decreasing demand for agricultural man power in proportion to the demand for industrial man power, only 21 per cent of the gainfully employed in 1930 were in agriculture.

That agricultural production will inevitably continue to increase in efficiency is evident from the current report of the National Resources Committee on *Technological Trends and National Policy*. The report states: "Few technologies available to agriculture have been utilized fully. Maximum efficiency in farm production has not been reached and is not in sight."[17] Even without new inventions, the spread through education of known techniques not now generally used will continue to increase produc-

---

[15] O. E. Baker, *The Outlook for Rural Youth*, Extension Service Circular 223 (U. S. Dept. of Agriculture, Washington, 1935), p. 2.

[16] D. Weintraub and I. Kaplan, *Summary of Findings to Date, March 1938*, Works Progress Administration, National Research Project (Philadelphia, Pa., March, 1938), p. 94.

[17] P. 97.

tivity per man, resulting in increasing displacement of agricultural labor. The only way to offset this decline would be to increase production markedly, and this is unlikely under the present trend toward production control and the current demands for agricultural products.

DEMAND FOR FOOD AND FEED PRODUCTS

The expansion of the domestic demand for agricultural products depends jointly upon population increase and expanded industrial use of these products. Since the bulk of agricultural products consists of foodstuffs and fibres, and since the per capita consumption of these articles changes very slowly, increase of population provides the surest increase in demand for the products of the commercial farmer. As long as the population was increasing both by births and vigorous immigration, there was a greater increase in demand for food than increase in productivity per man so that the number employed in agriculture was expanding. This increase was not as rapid, however, as that of employment in industry. In addition, the large-scale substitution of tractors for draft animals has markedly reduced the need for man power in production of crops to feed these animals.

The rate of population increase is now declining and a stationary population is predicted for the United States during the latter decades of this century. This means that the increase in output per man will inevitably overtake the slackening increase in population, so that the man-power needs of commercial agriculture for the production of foodstuffs will increase but slowly for a while and then gradually become stationary or even decline. There is some hope of postponing this decline through increasing per capita consumption of farm products, especially through manufacturing. This, however, would call not only for increased incomes for urban consumers but also for radical shifts in types of products, changes in consumption habits, and wider development of industrial uses for agricultural materials. If increased purchasing power can be placed in the hands of the ill-fed and poorly clothed, the farmers will be among the chief beneficiaries of their expanded buying. On the basis of the present trends and in consideration of the excess farm population already banked up, the report of the study of population redistribution estimates that "during the next 25 years . . . agriculture can make room for hardly more than one-fifth of the excess of farm births over deaths. . . ." [18]

THE FARMERS' PLIGHT IN THE NINETEEN-THIRTIES

The result of the precarious credit situation in the early years of the depression was a persistent pressure for farm debt relief, running the gamut from demands for moratoria to schemes for the federal government to underwrite the farm debt structure. Because of maladjustment in prices, increased dependence on cash crops, and a ballooning debt —the accumulation of years—the farmer found himself in a more desperate financial condition in the early nineteen-thirties than in any previous depression.

He felt the crushing force both of long-time factors directly causing agricultural distress and of the added effects of the industrial depression. In analyzing the agricultural situation the interdependence of agricultural and general economic prosperity is inescapably evident. As Bean and Chew have summed up the situation, "Facts about currencies, business conditions, industrial employment, wages,

---

[18] Carter Goodrich and Others, *Migration and Economic Opportunity* (Philadelphia, University of Pennsylvania Press, 1936), p. 407.

factory output, foreign tariffs, and consumer buying power matter quite as much as do strictly agricultural facts." [19] Only as industrial prosperity creates jobs for the surplus population and increases demands for the surplus raw materials can sound agricultural prosperity be achieved.

With superior land or management, farmers get by in hard times and clear a fair income in good times. However, with differentials in fertility and ability against them, a great mass of underprivileged farmers receives a meager income in good times and goes "in the red" in hard times. Although it is seldom realized or admitted, the national economy has been fostering rural slums as debased in their way as their city counterparts. In the prosperous year of 1929 nearly a million farms, 15 per cent of the total number in the United States, reported a gross production valued at less than $400. Nearly three million, or almost half of the farms in the country, reported a gross production valued at less than $1,000.[20]

Bearing in mind that these are gross income figures from which farming and living expenses must be deducted, it is apparent that in 1929 there was a class in agriculture consisting of from one to three million farmers whose level of living before the depression was far below what has been advocated as a minimum standard for health and decency and for whom any material diminution of income would mean serious want. It must also be considered that the figures represent gross income per farm and not per family and, in the case of a tenant farm, both the tenant's family and the landlord's family share in the income.

Makers of agricultural policies and programs have not

[19] Louis H. Bean and Arthur P. Chew, *Economic Trends Affecting Agriculture* (U. S. Dept. of Agriculture, Washington, 1933), p. 1.
[20] *Fifteenth Census of the United States: 1930*, Agriculture Vol. IV.

been clearly conscious of these submerged farmers. Most programs have been formulated for the "master" farmers on the mistaken theory that the disadvantaged farmers, who were often lacking in initiative as well as financial ability, would take advantage of the improved methods advocated. This they were unable to do. These latter farmers were in the lower income groups before 1929 and contributed heavily to the burden of rural relief during the nineteen-thirties. It is toward fundamental solution of their problems that programs should drive if they are to serve as preventives of future rural emergencies.

CHAPTER FOUR

MAN POWER AND OPPORTUNITY

FOR A NUMBER of years the teeming millions of the United States have increased mostly through the natural growth of the rural population. Farms and villages have provided not only their own increase but also much of the growth of cities and much of the human tide expanding the western frontier. The farm boy turned his face first westward, then cityward. For a time the expansion of industrial areas was so rapid that they not only absorbed millions of country-bred natives but also drew in aliens from the four corners of the earth. The farm, however, has been the chief source of man power since the early twenties. At that time European immigration was limited to definite quotas, and in recent years the usual immigrants who might have competed with native labor have been virtually barred. Today the out-movement and in-movement of migrants about balance each other, and the nation expands solely by excess of native births over deaths.

CHILDREN OF THE LAND

Although the general trend of the birth rate for the whole country has been downward for a century, the rate of natural increase has continued to be much higher in rural

districts than in cities. The rural birth rate has not declined to as low a level as the urban birth rate, and there
has been a great improvement in the rural death rate,
especially in the reduction of infant mortality, the limitation
of typhoid, and the rapid strides in the control of malaria
and tuberculosis. This has contributed to a continuing
excess of births over deaths, much greater in the rural than
in the city population. Recently, many American cities,
especially the large cities, have not maintained a balance of
births over deaths [1] and have drawn their increase in population from the bounteous supply of maturing farm youth.

Farm families have proportionately almost twice as many
children as city families,[2] and village families have over half
again as many. It is possible, on the basis of the number of
children and the prevailing death rates, to estimate fairly
accurately the rate at which various elements of the population will replace themselves.[3] On this basis, in the native
white population, city families have only about eight tenths
the required number necessary for replacement, village families slightly more than enough, and farm families nearly 50
per cent over replacement requirements.

Seemingly, the principle of lower birth rates among
more prosperous groups holds within the farm population
as well as within the industrial population. Not only was

---

[1] Leon E. Truesdell, "Trends in Urban Population," *The Municipal
Yearbook, 1937*, p. 132.

[2] T. J. Woofter, Jr., "The Natural Increase of the Rural Non-Farm
Population," *The Milbank Memorial Fund Quarterly*, Vol. xiii, No. 4
(1935), p. 314.

[3] On the basis of 1930 death rates.—Frank Lorimer and Frederick
Osborn, *Dynamics of Population*, Appendix (New York, The Macmillan
Co., 1934). On this basis 366 children under 5 per 1,000 women 15–44
are considered as 100 per cent replacement for the native white population. The 1930 urban population contained 292 children under 5 per
1,000 women 15–44, the rural-farm population 529, and the rural-nonfarm
population 463.

there a high rate of population production on the farm, but the rate was highest in the poorest farming districts. The lowest farm income areas—the Cotton South, the Appalachian Mountain Region, the Cut-Over Region of the Great Lakes, and the drought areas—stand out as the farm areas of greatest increase. The richer sections of New England, the Pacific Coast, and the Central States have low fertility rates. In fact, the fertility rate of large sections of the farm population of the Northeast is below the replacement level. If the poorest tenth of the counties of the United States is selected on the basis of lowest ranking in land values, in proportion of commercial products, and in standard of living, the counties falling in this disadvantaged group are also found to have the highest proportion of children.

Moreover, the higher than average birth rate for the rural population as a whole was accentuated in the relief group.[3a] In a special analysis of children in three hundred counties it was found that women twenty to forty-four years of age on relief had 25 per cent more children than the women in the rural population of the same counties. Hence, the next generation is being recruited heavily not only from the rural population but also from that portion of the rural population at the bottom of the economic ladder.

In spite of the high birth rate on the farms the number living there has not increased. The trend in migration to industry which was intensified in the first quarter of the twentieth century absorbed the rural excess. While the people living in cities and towns and, to a lesser extent, the people living in industrial villages, increased, the people

---

[3a] Carle C. Zimmerman and Nathan L. Whetten, *Rural Families on Relief*, Research Monograph XVII, Works Progress Administration, Division of Social Research (Washington, 1938), Chap. VII.

living on farms declined in number in spite of the high birth rate. In 1910 nearly twelve and a half million gainful workers were employed in agriculture and allied occupations, but by 1930 there had been a 15 per cent decrease to about ten and a half million. The loss was for the most part in "home" farm workers, indicating that while the number of families in agriculture remained almost stationary, the number of workers per family decreased. The proportion of gainful workers employed in agriculture fell from over one half of all workers in 1870 to about one fifth in 1930. As against this decrease in agriculture there was an increase of about 60 per cent in urban population. Thus, the ·rank and file of American city dwellers today are farm-bred.

Furthermore, just as the excess population increase was greatest in the poor land areas, so the migration to cities before 1930 was greatest out of these areas. Carter Goodrich in his exhaustive study of migration and economic opportunity analyzes the migratory trends of the past few decades in detail and concludes that "nothing in the entire analysis is more striking than the degree to which the migration of the twenties was drawing population away from those areas of chronic distress. . . ." [4]

Up to the industrial depression of the early nineteen-thirties, the pattern was set. There was an excess of population production on farms, particularly in areas where resources were least capable of supporting additional population and most pronouncedly among the poorer farm families, but the currents of migration flowed toward industrial centers and relieved the potential pressure on the land. The contraction of trade and industry beginning in 1929 violently disturbed this equilibrium. With the loss

---

[4] *Op. cit.*, p. 508.

of the drawing power of jobs, the flow to cities was dramatically curtailed. At the same time the trends of natural increase continued with little change.

DWINDLING OPPORTUNITY

The most fundamental reversal in population trends during the depression years came from the virtual cessation of net movement from farm to city. Whereas the net gain of cities from rural districts resulted in the steady draining-off of the rural excess before 1930, the cessation of industrial opportunity cut the net gain down to about six hundred thousand people from 1930 through 1934,[5] or an average of only one hundred and twenty thousand per year. In one year, 1932, the movement to farms actually exceeded the movement from farms. In a sense, it is deceptive to concentrate attention on the net movement cityward during the thirties since it was the final result of a considerable shifting of population in both directions: a total of millions moving to farms from cities, towns, and villages and other millions moving to cities, towns, and villages from farms.[6] Since the currents to the city did not always originate in the places to which the currents from the city flowed, there was a considerable shifting of farm population. While the poor land areas were havens for the jobless, some of the good land areas continued to send out migrants. As the migrants varied by age and by geographic sections, the resultant population changes were unevenly distributed and intensified the problems of rural areas in which the population already exceeded opportunity.

---

[5] *Farm Population Estimates, January 1, 1937* (U. S. Dept. of Agriculture, Bureau of Agricultural Economics, Washington, release of June 24, 1937).
[6] *Ibid.*

By 1936 the net movement from farms had picked up some momentum again and was the largest since 1929. As a result there were fewer persons on farms on January 1, 1937, than in either 1934, 1935, or 1936. The 1936 net loss of eighty thousand persons meant little, however, in terms of the excess pressure on the land, since the increase in the male working population on farms amounts to more than two hundred thousand per year.

CONCENTRATION OF POPULATION ON POOR LAND

Since the rate of natural increase of population was heaviest in the poorest agricultural areas, the maturing population which would have moved out had opportunity been present piled up faster than in other places. There was also some tendency for the reverse movement of discouraged city people to be heavier back to these depressed areas than to the better farming areas. Complicating still further the problem of population pressure on agricultural resources was the fact that a number of stranded rural dwellers who had been engaged in mining, lumbering, or other nonfarm activities shifted, as soon as the depression threw them out of work, to subsistence farming to produce food for their families. Many were unsuccessful. In February, 1935, 12 per cent of the rural workers on relief whose usual occupation had been nonagricultural had shifted to agriculture, as against about 1 per cent whose usual occupation was agriculture who had changed to nonagricultural occupations.[7] This shift was more pronounced in the cut-over region around the Great Lakes and in the Appalachian Mountains than in other regions. In those two areas 22 per cent and 25 per cent, respectively, of the relief clients

---

[7] Survey of Current Changes in the Rural Relief Population, Division of Social Research, Works Progress Administration, Washington, D. C.

with previous nonagricultural occupations were currently employed in agriculture. Thus, because of the more rapid natural increase of population, the heavier movement back from cities, and the tendency to shift from unprofitable rural industries to farming, there was an unusual strain on agriculture in the regions least able to support it.

The effect of the discontinuance of most of the outward movement plus the effect of a back flow into the Appalachian Mountains is revealed by a recent study of four Appalachian counties. "The gains in farm population [from 1930 to 1935] were considerable, amounting to 49 per cent in Haywood County, N. C., 31 per cent in Avery County, N. C., 16 per cent in Magoffin County, Ky., and 14 per cent in Morgan County, Ky. But while there was a general increase in the number of farms in these areas, the acreage devoted to agricultural purposes expanded only slightly in Avery and Haywood, remained unchanged in Morgan, and actually contracted in Magoffin. Inaccessibility, roughness, and low fertility worked together to render the amount of land available for farming decidedly inflexible. The increase in farm population, unaccompanied by any expansion in farm acreage, resulted in the greatest congestion ever known in these counties, thus producing deplorable housing conditions and unprecedented 'doubling up' among families." [8]

MATURING LABORERS

Many of the troubles of the nineteen-thirties were related to this unequal growth of the population. When attention is focussed on the working ages (eighteen to sixty-five

---

[8] L. S. Dodson, *Living Conditions and Population Migration in Four Appalachian Counties*, Social Research Report No. III (U. S. Dept. of Agriculture, Washington, October, 1937), p. 1.

years), it is apparent that the most rapid increases were in this element.

Without careful analysis it would seem anomalous that, after a ten-year fairly steady fall in the birth rate, the United States in the early nineteen-thirties should have experienced the heaviest expansion in its laboring population. Although births began to decline in actual number after 1921, this decline was slight up to 1924. While such a trend slackens the increase in the total population, it does not affect the labor market until children reach the age of maturity and seek jobs. The number who pass the age of eighteen every year will continue to increase up to 1939–42 and will decline rather rapidly thereafter; that is, the increase in births up to 1924 will continue for eighteen years to effect an increase in persons over eighteen years of age.

In the early nineteen-thirties, when industrial opportunity was at a low ebb, the population was already receiving nearly the maximum increase in persons of employable age. The number of males eighteen to sixty-five years of age increased by over three million from 1930 through 1935, and during the same period a like number of maturing young women became potential entrants into employment. Of this increase nearly two fifths were in the farm population. This increase of employable persons at a time when industry was least able to absorb them was one of the chief reasons why the numbers applying for public relief continued to mount even though industrial employment improved steadily.

The progressive shifting of population from the high-birth-rate rural areas to the low-birth-rate urban areas, which occurs in periods of industrial prosperity, is a major factor in the declining natural increase of the American population. Those who are primarily interested in a healthy increase in the population have gone so far as to advocate an extensive back-to-the-land movement. Whether this by itself would check the rapid decline in the birth rate is problematical.

In this matter of the arithmetic of population and agricultural production there is a dilemma for the nation in general and rural families in particular. It is calculated that roughly three children per fertile couple are necessary to insure an increasing population. Two of them are required to replace their parents, and the third to offset childless people and allow for increase. Since only one couple is needed to replace the present farm population, the third child will be in excess of present opportunities. It is this excess above two children per farm family which must seek new farms or migrate to centers of industrial opportunity.

Here the excess rural population faces another dilemma. Approximately 50 per cent of the present farmers produce 90 per cent of the commercial crops, and the tendency toward concentration of commercial production is growing with the increasing mechanization of agriculture. The other farmers are largely dependent on subsistence agriculture and receive little cash income from their farm enterprises. Their production could be entirely cut off without materially reducing the volume of crops which moves in the channels of trade.

From the viewpoint of industrial labor the excess mass of underemployed low-wage agricultural population is a menace. In areas such as the South, where population pressure is great, industrial wages tend to remain low because farm boys will accept any rate of pay slightly above the pittance returned by agriculture. This has operated to keep the South a land of cheap and easily exploited human power.

THE FUTURE WORKING POPULATION

It is revealing to note the location of children now born and to calculate their future effect on the labor market as they mature and seek work. The babies of 1937 will be eighteen years old by 1955. Without any speculation on the future course of the birth rate we can, by applying the death rate, predict the growth in man power up to 1955.

Let us further assume that the people now on farms will stay on farms, that those now in villages will stay in villages, and that those now in cities will stay in cities. This we know will not be the case but if we picture such a situation without migration it enables us to visualize the magnitude and direction of the movement which will be necessary to maintain balance in the labor supply.

With this assumption and the further condition that foreign immigration will remain negligible, the United States will have over the next eighteen years an increase in the working ages (eighteen to sixty-five years) of over 7,000,000 on farms, 4,000,000 in villages, and 3,000,000 in cities, a total increase of over 14,000,000 in the number of people of employable age. On the basis of the 1930 proportion, approximately 65 per cent will seek work; that is, 9,000,000 new workers must be cared for by the expansion of agriculture and industry over and above the 9,000,000 unemployed in 1937.

Since the overwhelming majority of these boys and girls are growing up in farm and village homes, it is evidently futile to expect great relief for the unemployed in the cities through a back-to-the-farm movement. An already burdened agriculture has no room for the farm increase and stability is to be expected not from a back-to-the-farm movement but from the opposite trend.

Most of this increase in the working population will occur in the early part of the period. By 1950 the city working population (if not swelled by migrants) will decline, that of the villages will be stationary, and the farm increase will be markedly slower. This means that the most pressing problems will arise within the next ten years.

The problem of overpopulation in poor land areas can ultimately be solved. The slackening rate of population increase will help to reduce the pressure on the land in the future, and, to the extent that artificial methods of family limitation spread to rural areas, this decline in pressure will be accelerated. Industry will again draw upon the vigorous maturing rural population. But for the next two decades, lacking success in the spreading of commercial production among more farmers and in the stimulation of a high standard of production for home use, there will be a large depressed farm population living in normal times in precarious insecurity and in times of depression on relief.

In areas of excess population production relief loads piled up, due not so much to the size of families as to the occurrence of this excess in areas of limited opportunity. Since the trend of the birth rate indicates a continuance of this population tendency, it is evident that, when in the future the channels of migration are again blocked, relief will be the alternative for stranded rural people.

It is this maladjustment of population to opportunity which, as much as the economic depression, lies at the root of the difficulty in reducing unemployment, of the problems of youth, of the difficulty in climbing the agricultural ladder to ownership, and of the handicaps of rural institutions and services for equalizing opportunity. Many of the conditions described in succeeding chapters must therefore be projected against this situation.

CHAPTER FIVE

PERPLEXED YOUTH

THE EXISTENCE of a mass youth problem has only recently been realized and the particular difficulties of farm youth have hardly received the attention which they deserve. Coming of age on a farm during the depression of the nineteen-thirties involved unprecedented dilemmas. It has been pointed out that entry into agriculture has been growing more difficult, that the depression made entry into industry almost impossible, and that during the period of contracting agriculture and stagnant industry there was an annual increase of more than two hundred thousand in the farm males of working age. On the threshold of productive life, at the age of readiest adaptation to work and to family and community life, youth of this generation faced an economy which, at least temporarily, did not need them. Nothing short of a sharp expansion in industrial and agricultural employment will absorb the steady increase of new workers which is being piled on top of the supply of older workers who are unemployed. Lacking an expanding economy, American youth will no longer be stimulated by the ambition to strive boldly.

In the past, young men and women reared on farms or in villages had several courses open to them: they could

follow agriculture into new lands, they could seek their
fortune in the city, or they could stay at home to succeed
their parents on the farm.

YOUTH AND MIGRATION

Up to the turn of the century the boy who did not wish
to stay at home and wrestle with the perplexities of becoming a landowner had only to move west in order to get
free land as a result of the government's public land policy.
After a period of pioneering he could expect civilization to
reach his outpost with resulting increases in land values and
community services. But there is no more free land and
pioneering has ceased to be a quick way to independent
ownership. The covered wagon no longer provides relief
from population pressure.

In the years after 1930 cities offered few employment
opportunities, and there was literally no place for rural
youth to go. Young people maturing on the farm during
the depression were forced to stay at home where there
were at least shelter and a minimum of food, even though
there was no work for them to do and even though their
families were often dependent for their livelihood on government assistance.

American industry has expanded and American cities
have prospered by means of the constant renewal of youth
and vigor from farm homes. Between 1920 and 1930 some
two million farm youth moved to cities. The greatest part
of this movement went to metropolitan centers—a fourth
of it into only four metropolitan areas, those of New
York, Chicago, Detroit, and Los Angeles. A few large
industrial areas began absorbing much of the maturing
youth of the whole country. In this mass movement girls
left the farms at an earlier age than boys, and more young

people left the poorer agricultural areas than the better farm lands.

From 1930 through 1934 there was a total cityward movement of only two hundred thousand in the five years, as contrasted with an average of two hundred thousand per year between 1920 and 1930. This slowing down of the migration of youth to one fifth of its previous normal volume caused a piling up of young people in farm homes which had widespread repercussions. Between 1930 and 1935 the number of rural youth increased by over a million while the number of city-born youth was approaching the stationary level. Farm youth increased faster than village youth.

Not only were the channels of migration blocked by the effect of the depression but also the usual rural opportunities were dried up. All the adverse conditions described in previous chapters which were operating as a drag on agriculture have also operated as obstacles to the entrance into agriculture by youth either as farmers or as laborers. Farm ownership, that "top of the ladder" to which youth remaining on the land formerly aspired to climb, has with the intensification of adverse conditions become increasingly difficult of attainment except through inheritance. The trend had been in operation for some time, but the depression brought it into clear perspective.

EMPLOYMENT OF YOUTH

Ordinarily, the most significant shift of youthful employment within agriculture occurs between the ages of twenty and thirty. In that period the majority of youth in agriculture are laborers; afterwards the majority are owners or tenants. The number of laborers above thirty years of age remains fairly constant except for the normal decrease due to death, which indicates that, if the shift out of the laboring class has not been made by that age, laborer becomes more or less a lifetime status.

For those who have shifted from farm labor to tenancy the added step to ownership has also become more difficult. With the exhaustion of free land, the increase in land values, the increase in capital needs, and adverse agricultural prices, ownership has been declining since 1910 rather than increasing. Thus each step up the agricultural ladder has become progressively more difficult to take.

The greatest outlet for the dammed up energy of young people has been in home farm chores. Whereas the trend before 1930 was toward a decrease in home farm labor, from 1930 to 1935 home farm employment more than doubled.[1] Work on the home farm is classed as an occupation more as a matter of statistics than of reality. Those so classed by the census are unpaid. Some are really needed at home to help with the farm chores but the majority are merely staying at home for shelter and contributing such help as they can for their keep until some gainful employment opens up. By and large it is wasted man power. How cheaply it is held is indicated by an advertisement in a farm paper in April, 1937, when the agricultural situation was improving, which offered a white youth, as payment for farm work, his room, board, and laundry, and $2.50 per week.

This, then, is an economic dilemma of first magnitude—rural-farm boys increasing at the rate of about two hundred thousand per year in excess of the number necessary to replace deaths and retirement among the workers above eighteen years of age. At the threshold of productive life

---

[1] *United States Census of Agriculture: 1935.*

this generation is confronted with restricted industrial opportunity and contracting agricultural opportunity.

The situation for village youth while precarious has not been quite as desperate as that of farm youth. Pressure for jobs is not quite so severe, since youth make up a slightly smaller proportion of the total rural-nonfarm than of the farm population. In the dominantly agricultural states where villages are primarily trading centers for the surrounding farm area, problems of farm and nonfarm youth are closely akin. In primarily industrial states, however, where the majority of rural youth are nonfarm, the problems of village youth often are more like those of city youth.

Whereas in the past farm youth expected ultimately to cultivate their own acres, village youth expected to own a business or to attain a secure position in some profession or skilled trade. Into this traditional scheme of things has come the development of lumbering, mining, textile, and other rural industries. More and more have village youth come to enter these occupations as laborers, dependent on a daily wage. The labor market in such industries is not expanding, however, and depleted natural resources and technological advances have actually reduced labor requirements in many nonagricultural industries in rural areas. There is already an adequate supply of experienced labor in the older ages for the jobs which are available.

RELIEF YOUTH

Some youth, impatient with idleness under the parental rooftree, have taken to the road. At one time the transient relief population included as many as two hundred thousand individuals and fifty thousand family groups, and it has been estimated that two to three times that number at some time or other belonged to the wandering class. About one fifth of the unattached transients were from rural areas. Examination of records of the depression wanderers showed that there were many causes which had made transients of rural people who formerly had homes: the shutting down of mines, layoffs in factories and small businesses, as well as crop failures and the inability of parents to provide support. At least two fifths, and in some months almost one half, of the unattached transients were between sixteen and twenty-four years of age. All types of young people made up these hordes of wanderers, including children of farmers, miners, and factory workers, as well as college students and white-collar workers.[2]

That the majority stayed at home, however, is indicated by the large number of rural youth in the relief population. Some two million of the persons in relief households during the great depression were from sixteen through twenty-four years of age. For the most part, these did not come directly to relief agencies as only 13 per cent were recorded as the economic heads of their families. The other 87 per cent were dependent members of families whose heads could not support their households.[3]

Under ordinary demands for labor these youth would have secured employment and made their contribution to the family budget. They found themselves doubly disadvantaged in that they were not only unable to obtain employment but were also forced to remain in households whose heads were not self-supporting.

---

[2] John N. Webb, *The Transient Unemployed*, Research Monograph III, Works Progress Administration, Division of Social Research (Washington, 1935).

[3] Bruce L. Melvin, *Rural Youth on Relief*, Research Monograph XI, Works Progress Administration, Division of Social Research (Washington, 1937), Table, p. 80.

In order to know the characteristics of these doubly disadvantaged youth, a study was made of rural youth in relief
households in the United States in February, 1935, when
the peak load of 1,370,000 youth was reached. Of these,
almost one out of every three lived in a village. Those
living in the open country were not necessarily on farms.
Relief youth were about equally divided between boys and
girls, with a slightly larger number of the latter.

The employment status and experience of rural youth
in relief households indicates to what a large extent they
have been the victims of lack of economic opportunity.
Almost two out of every five boys sixteen through twenty-
four years of age were working, but at insufficient wages.
Another two fifths were looking for work. Most of the
remainder were still in school, often because they could find
no work. Only one out of every three girls was working
or looking for work outside of the home.

Most of the boys and girls who were looking for work
had had some sort of temporary job, but this often had
lasted for only a few months. In all too many cases previous employment experience had meant working on the
home farm without a cash wage. Those who had worked
off the farm had usually held unskilled jobs. Most of the
girls who had had any sort of nonagricultural job had been
servants. The fact that four out of every five rural boys
and girls in relief households who had had jobs had done
work that called for no special training is a sad commentary
on the lack of special training and skills among rural youth.
Among the boys, only one in every nine had been a farm
operator and nearly all of these had been share croppers or
other tenants.

Those fortunate enough to have secured a job were
markedly underemployed. The jobs paid very little or

offered only part-time employment so that the youth could not help to raise their families above relief status. As might be expected, those with employment were predominantly farm laborers, a few were trying unsuccessfully to operate farms, and a few others had unskilled jobs off the farm. Also, many of those classified as farm laborers belonged to that unpaid family labor group which bulks so large among rural youth today. These while not strictly unemployed are markedly underemployed.

EDUCATION

One method of helping to solve the unemployment problem of the increasing surplus of youth, which is widely advocated, is a longer educational period. Despite the growing sentiment for keeping as large a portion as possible of youth under eighteen years of age in school, this goal is far from attainment in rural-farm families. The school attendance of youth sixteen and seventeen years old in the farm population is a little over 50 per cent as against over 60 per cent in the city.

One favorable effect of the depression, however, has been the tendency to prolong school attendance. Lacking the pull of jobs and encouraged by aid from youth agencies, many youth have remained in high school or gone on to college who otherwise would have cut their education short. School systems have had a record enrollment in a period of restricted budgets.

The general lack of adequate educational facilities in many rural areas is intensified with respect to youth since high schools are even less readily available than are elementary schools. The lack of high schools is most serious in areas with the greatest surplus of rural youth. Poor land areas have the least money to spend on schools in spite of

CCC

Youth Working on Federal Project

FSA, USDA

A Rural School

the use of a large proportion of their incomes for education.

Because of inadequacy of facilities rural youth not only attend school to a lesser extent than urban youth but they also leave school earlier on the average, complete fewer grades, and have a higher rate of retardation. Rural-farm youth are more handicapped in all of these respects than are rural-nonfarm youth, while relief youth are the most disadvantaged class of all. In every group boys receive less formal education than girls.

Illiteracy also remains a serious problem. As late as 1930 about one out of every twenty rural-farm youth in the United States was still unable to read and write.[4] The proportions of illiterate youth were particularly high in the states with a large surplus of youth and with large numbers of Negro and Mexican youth.

While school facilities are gradually improving, farm youth will always have the handicap of transportation. In many sections complete lack of adequate transportation facilities makes school attendance at a distance impractical. Even when facilities are available, distance remains a factor in the situation. Yet the indications are that when rural youth have the opportunity a large proportion attend school. Hence, it may be assumed that with increased facilities a substantial increase in rural school attendance will result.

Increased educational opportunities for rural youth must unquestionably be in the direction of expanded facilities for vocational training. One of the factors in the desperate economic plight of many rural youth is the fact that they have neither employment experience nor skills to offer in

---

[4] *Fifteenth Census of the United States: 1930*, Population Vol. II.

the labor market.   Large numbers of untrained rural youth cannot hope to secure anything but the most menial type of employment.   Even where vocational education is available, it is chiefly limited to agriculture and home economics.   Nonagricultural training for farm youth who cannot go into the already overcrowded agricultural field and for all rural-nonfarm youth is urgently needed if they are to enter the labor market on terms that will enable them to compete with older workers.   Any program of vocational education should also include vocational guidance as rural youth have practically no opportunities, unaided, to know where employment opportunities exist or to determine the qualifications required for occupations available outside of their limited local areas.   At present, the agencies for vocational guidance are practically inoperative in rural areas.

Because such large numbers of rural youth eventually become residents of cities, and must do so if cities are to maintain or increase their present populations, their education is important to urban as well as rural areas.   To the extent that they are educating youth who will eventually migrate, rural areas are making an important contribution to urban areas.   Hence, for the benefit of urban as well as rural areas there must be a general leveling up of educational opportunity.   To accomplish this effectively federal participation is essential.   A start has been made in the allocation of federal funds for vocational training in agriculture and home economics, but far more extensive participation by the national government in the financing of public education is needed.   In terms of the economic and social welfare of the general population, no investment will yield greater returns.   If this investment is not made the present generation is definitely handicapped.

MARITAL AND SOCIAL ADJUSTMENTS

Besides being the period of educational, migratory, and occupational adjustments, youth is also the age of marital and social adjustments. Rural youth as a group marry earlier than urban youth. Since the bulk of all marriages occurs within this youth group, the depression decrease in the marriage rate was due primarily to the postponement of marriage among young people. It is questionable whether there was much of a decline among the farm groups of certain areas and among many rural-nonfarm groups, so that most of the delayed marriages of young people were apparently in the urban population. Even this decline was only temporary so that as far as marriage is concerned the problems of rural youth appear to be not so much those of delay as of difficulty in providing that minimum economic base which is so essential to future security and happiness.

The social adjustments of youth are closely related to their recreational opportunities. Aside from the mechanized and commercialized pleasures afforded by the automobile, the motion picture, and the radio, rural areas have been slow to realize the social needs of youth and have been even slower to make provision for meeting them. Where rural organizations and institutions do exist, a large proportion of youth do not participate in them. In fact it is the youth in the lowest economic groups and with the least education, those youth who are already severely handicapped, who participate least in recreational activities of any type. Moreover, the lack of such facilities is most acute in poor land areas, those areas where all the problems of youth are intensified.

Youth is a period of adaptation and adjustment. It is the period of occupational choice, often involving migration, a period of family establishment and of formation of community ties. Conditions increasing the difficulties of youth in getting a start are likely to be lifelong in their effects. To the extent that the various adverse conditions confronting youth are not alleviated, the depression will leave a lasting imprint on the next generation.

CHAPTER SIX

UNEQUAL OPPORTUNITIES

AMERICAN DEMOCRACY was founded on the principle of equal opportunity for all. Throughout the history of the country equality of opportunity has resounded as a political slogan, but the evolution of the nation has inevitably brought about variations in the accessibility of public services. In many areas the marked deficiency of opportunity for large classes of the population is the result of social and economic handicaps which are glaringly apparent when the disadvantages of these areas and classes are contrasted with the advantages of those areas and classes for whom ample opportunity does exist. What is true on a broad scale for the nation as a whole is painfully true for rural areas. Because of the concentration of profits in financial centers, rural areas have not had the means to keep up with the cities in providing those facilities which make for a satisfactory standard of living. Among the essentials upon whose existence opportunity for the great mass of the population directly depends are educational and library provisions and health services. Equally as important is the whole range of communication facilities—telephones, newspapers, magazines, radios. Not only are the rural districts as a whole disadvantaged in comparison with cities but also the disadvantages are intensified in those rural areas in which economic and social handicaps are multiplying.

SCHOOL AND LIBRARY FACILITIES

The inequalities between country schools and city schools in length of term and expenditures per pupil have been written about too extensively to call for elaboration here. The one-room schoolhouse of the farm community has too often remained just that while its city counterpart has acquired kindergartens, shops, gymnasiums, and laboratories. The country often has only a grade school to set against the city's junior high school, commercial high school, trade school, and normal school; and some municipalities even support colleges. The tragic inequality of opportunity which results for the rural boy or girl is self-evident. Consolidation of rural schools, where practicable, is tending to alleviate the situation in many states, but that alone is not always enough.[1] Hand in hand with consolidation must go greatly expanded school equipment, liberalization of curricula, and increased teaching efficiency.

The disparity between urban and rural areas is succinctly stated in a report of the Advisory Committee on Education: "In 1935–36 almost equal numbers of children were attending city schools and rural schools. City school systems spent an average of $108 that year for each child in attendance; rural schools spent an average of $67. Since town and village schools are counted as rural for statistical purposes, average expenditures per child in schools of open-country areas were undoubtedly much lower than $67.

"Low school expenditures in rural areas have unfortunate

---

[1] Dwight Sanderson, *Research Memorandum on Rural Life in the Depression*, Bulletin 34 (New York, Social Science Research Council, 1937), pp. 83–90.

results for the children. Since the teachers are poorly paid, they are frequently untrained and inexperienced. They usually follow textbooks and make little use of supplementary materials to give vitality and interest to their teaching. School terms average a month shorter than in cities. The health, welfare, guidance, and other services that school children need in addition to instruction are almost universally lacking.

"In 1930, 800,000 children in the United States between the ages of 7 and 13 were not going to school at all. Most of these children lived in the poorest rural areas, where relief problems have been most serious since 1930." [2]

The disparity in educational opportunity between rural and urban areas, always present, becomes even greater in periods of depression. In comparing the situation in 140 agricultural villages in 1936 with that in 1930, Brunner and Lorge noted a marked shortening of school terms and shrinkage in teachers' salaries.[3] In fact, had it not been for the emergency education program of the federal government many teachers would have been virtually on relief. Nearly 2,000 rural schools in twenty-four states failed to open in the fall of 1933 because of lack of funds. This deprived 100,000 children of educational opportunity.

Deficiency of opportunity is closely associated with relief needs. Lack of education and training shows up in the lower school accomplishments of the relief as compared with the nonrelief population. In one comparison relief families were found to have had distinctly less schooling than their self-supporting neighbors. The proportion of

---

[2] The Advisory Committee on Education, *The Federal Government and Education* (Washington, 1938), pp. 2–3.

[3] Edmund deS. Brunner and Irving Lorge, *Rural Trends in Depression Years* (New York, Columbia University Press, 1937).

relief family heads who had never attended school was more than double the proportion of the heads of neighboring households not receiving relief, and almost double for those who had not progressed as far as the fifth grade—for those, that is, who had achieved little more than the bare ability to read and write. Less than one half of the heads of relief households, as compared with two thirds of their self-supporting neighbors, had completed eight grades or more. Lack of training and opportunity is also indicated in the fact that farm laborers, croppers, and rural unskilled laborers contributed more than their proportionate share to the relief burden.

These variations were observable not only for the economic heads of households in rural areas but also for their children. Children in relief households were found to be consistently at a disadvantage with respect to school attainment in comparison with those in nonrelief households. In one survey three fifths of the children twelve to nineteen years of age in nonrelief households were found to have completed grade school, as compared with less than one half of those in relief households, and the disparity was even greater among those of high school age. Thus, this neglect of rural schools has levied on society the cost of relief for those not able to meet their emergencies, and any saving on education will in the long run have to be paid for in other social costs.

Closely allied to the functions of the schools in meeting the educational needs of rural areas are those of libraries. According to a recent estimate over 70 per cent of the rural population has no library service except the questionable amount available through school libraries.[4] With the in-

---

[4] *Report of the Advisory Committee on Education* (Washington, 1938)

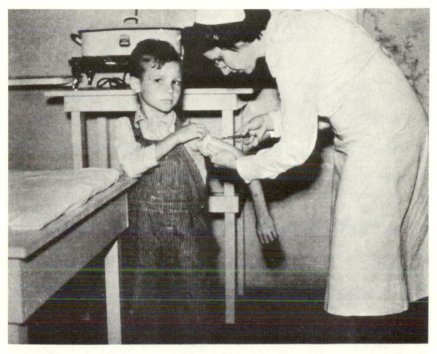

A Rural Clinic

Saddlebag Library

creasing awareness of the need for recreational facilities as well as for expanded educational opportunities, the place of the library in rural life must receive increased emphasis.

PUBLIC HEALTH SERVICES

In rural public health programs, as in education and library service, there is much to be desired. Communicable diseases are not sufficiently controlled in rural areas. Control has lagged far behind city standards because the need is not so obvious as in crowded urban areas as well as because funds are lacking for an adequate program. As a result typhoid has become largely a rural disease. Malaria is most prevalent in the open country. Pellagra is associated almost entirely with rural dietary deficiencies. The rate of preventable deaths, especially in maternity cases, and among infants under one year of age is still disproportionately high among farm families.

Much of this loss is attributable to the lag in public health programs in the poorer areas. While relatively adequate standards for public health needs involve the provision of a hospital in nearly every county and a public health nurse to every 2,000 people, recent surveys showed over 1,300 counties without a registered general hospital and some counties with as many as 25,000 people per nurse.[5] At the beginning of 1935 only about one sixth of the counties had health units.

Ill-health is a potent factor in poverty. The high proportion of those persons in rural areas who fail to make a living as a result of physical deficiency is directly attributable to lack of public health facilities, hospitals, and physicians' services. In some commercial crop areas the diets of the

---

[5] National Health Conference, *Report of the Committee on Medical Care* (Washington, 1938), pp. 19, 31.

laborers and croppers are so meager and unbalanced as to impair efficiency and vigor. In such areas a large proportion of the costs of rural relief goes for medical attention. In many cases marginal families which do not go on relief are actually worse off than relief families since their own funds for health services, always below needs, are still further reduced.

In evaluating the whole problem of adequate provision for education and public health in rural areas it is necessary to emphasize that in times of budget trimming the heaviest cuts fall on these services. The functions of the courts and other governmental services and public works are maintained at as high a level as possible, imposing almost the whole brunt of economy upon public welfare institutions at the very time when the need for the services of these institutions is greatest.

CONTRIBUTIONS OF RURAL AREAS

Since the farms are producing the next generation and maturing youth for the nation's labor supply, institutions for promoting public welfare are of particular importance in the open country. Although it is in the rural states in general that such institutions are weakest, yet it is upon their efficiency that the quality of our future population largely depends.

The welfare of the people of the United States cannot be considered in compartments bounded by state lines. The restless tides of movement toward areas of expanding economic opportunity and away from areas of static opportunity have always overflowed state lines, welding the labor supply of the nation into a unit. The early movements toward land opportunity were southward, then westward, draining some of the young people first from New England farms, and then from farms of the Middle States and the South. Early in this century a pronounced reverse movement set in toward the industrial opportunities of the Northeastern and the Middle Atlantic States.

This movement from agriculture to industry has, in recent decades, been one of the chief internal migratory trends. Future increases in the industrial demand for labor will increase this flow. Formerly this demand was partially supplied by millions of foreign immigrants. The continued restriction of European immigration will intensify the interdependence of the native agricultural and industrial populations.

Recently California has been the greatest importer of people. Between 1920 and 1930 the in-movement of persons born elsewhere was nearly one million two hundred thousand greater than the number of California-born who moved to other states. Five northeastern states and Florida received over one hundred thousand more natives of other states than the total of their own native-born who left their borders. The states of the South and West exported heavily both in actual numbers and in proportion to their total populations.

A glance at the areas producing population and those affording industrial opportunity is all that is necessary to convince one that this shifting of population will continue. The states with ample opportunities do not have a sufficiently large young population markedly to increase their present labor supply. States with predominantly agricultural economies have large excess youth populations. States with natural increase rates of over 10 per 1,000 [6] in 1930

---

[6] *Birth, Stillbirth, and Infant Mortality Statistics for the Birth Registration Area of the United States 1930* (U. S. Dept. of Commerce, Bureau of the Census, Washington).

were Alabama, Arkansas, Idaho, Kentucky, Mississippi, New Mexico, North Carolina, North Dakota, South Carolina, Utah, Virginia, West Virginia, and Wyoming. These high increase states are largely rural. The agricultural states rear the population; the industrial states provide the expanding demand for labor. Thus normally there is a constant flow to the industrial states.

The import states are receiving their labor supply from other training centers. It is to their advantage to secure well-trained and well-balanced individuals, such as are produced only in communities with well-developed public services, including educational, public health, and public welfare institutions. This is another reason for the vital need in backward communities for the development of all programs concerned with the welfare of children and young people.

The constant influx of people from underprivileged areas into the cities creates problems for industry and for city institutions. The adaptation of rural Negroes and mountain people to the industrial labor market is a constant source of trouble to employers, on the one hand, and to labor leaders, on the other. Public health and welfare institutions are strained by the presence of such groups unused to city ways, and the proportion of seriously retarded children which they bring into the schools calls for great care in adjustment. These children must be brought up to normal educational achievement or their presence in large numbers will divert opportunity and attention from pupils of already normal advancement.

Few besides the technical students of population realize the burden imposed on communities which rear a population for the benefit of productive enterprise in other communities. Children must be supported by people in the productive ages, and migration is steadily draining these away.

The predominant age of first migration is from twenty to forty-five, and this sends a disproportionately large number of productive people to industrial communities and leaves, of course, a disproportionately large number of the young behind in the agricultural communities. States with large proportions of their populations within the ages twenty-one through sixty-four years are California, Illinois, Massachusetts, Missouri, Nevada, New Jersey, New York, Ohio, Oregon, and Washington, all with over 55.7 per cent within these ages. The states with less than 50 per cent in the productive age group are Alabama, Arkansas, Georgia, Kentucky, Mississippi, New Mexico, North Carolina, North Dakota, Oklahoma, South Carolina, Tennessee, Utah, Virginia, and West Virginia.

In the rural states one third and more of the population is of school age; in the industrial states, one fourth and under. In an effort to arrive at the money value for the services rendered in the rearing of children it has been estimated that each mature individual represents an outlay of from $2,000 to $3,000. Accepting the average figure of $2,500, this amount, although small for each individual, represents a heavy contribution in the aggregate through the migrants to cities. It has been estimated that in the next twenty years over 7,000,000 more boys and girls on farms will mature past the eighteenth year than are necessary to replace their parents. A fair proportion of these will migrate to industrial centers; on the basis of past experience 4,750,000 is a very conservative figure. On this assumption, at a cost of $2,500 apiece for rearing and educating them up to eighteen years, rural areas will contribute nearly $12,000,000,000 to industrial areas. At the rate of present expenditures about one fifth of this, or $2,500,000,000, will be paid for the elementary schooling of these children from public taxes. No allowance is made in this estimate for public health or other services. This estimate is doubly conservative because it is based on the number who will pass the age of eighteen, whereas, for each one hundred who attain that age approximately ten die between one and eighteen years of age. The cost of those who do not reach maturity has not been considered.

When the rate of production of this increase in the working population is compared with per capita income, there is an almost perfect correspondence of the low income states with those of high population increase. The heaviest cost of supplying the future labor market falls on the states with the smallest per capita wealth and the lowest proportion of wage earners. These are also debtor states which must secure their capital from financial centers.

THE TAX BASE

Thus, the financing of rural institutions for the promotion of the public welfare in backward rural communities becomes one of primary significance to the nation as a whole. Failure to provide adequate facilities is almost entirely due to lack of money and not to lack of willingness. It has been shown in a number of studies of public finance that the states with backward facilities are taxing themselves more heavily per dollar of wealth than the more advanced states, even though they are still not producing the revenue necessary for extensive modern institutions.

A recent report of the National Education Association points out that, while the farm population earns about 9 per cent of the nation's income, it is responsible, except as aided from other sources, such as state school funds, for financing the education of 31 per cent of the nation's children.[7] The report further points out that according to reliable estimates of tax resources the tax revenues per child range from $50 or less in six of the southern rural states to $200 or more in eight of the industrial states. The intense concentration of economic power in certain states, and especially in the cities of these states, leaves the backward rural areas greatly disadvantaged, and, unless they are aided by the redistribution of tax funds, they are destined to become more so.

Any honest facing of the facts about excess proportions in the dependent ages and deficient taxable wealth for support of institutions shows the necessity for the use of the broader tax base of the states and the nation in order to achieve some sort of equalization of funds between urban and rural areas. Some states have approached this problem with educational equalization funds guaranteeing minimum salaries and school terms for all school districts. Without similar grants-in-aid made by the federal government on the basis of need and size of youthful population, many of the agricultural states are inescapably handicapped in the promotion of general education. Likewise the federal government must participate to an increasing extent in the field of rural health if adequate prevention and curative facilities are to be generally available.

Levy of taxes by the federal government on wealth where it is located and expenditure of money to meet need where it exists are two of the most painless and efficient forms of wealth redistribution. In practice they make possible a more equitable development of the areas which condition

---

[7] "Population Trends and Their Educational Implications," *Research Bulletin of the National Education Association*, Vol. XVI, No. 1 (Washington, January, 1936), p. 46.

the future generations of the whole nation. Furthermore, they are the only methods by which rural-urban relative equality of opportunity can be effected.

UNDERPRIVILEGED CHILDREN

It should be emphasized that while the lack of job opportunities bears heavily on the youth group, the inequality in services between rich and poor areas and advantaged and disadvantaged classes disinherits an army of children from society's benefits.

A canvass by the visiting teachers of a single state showed that there were twenty-five thousand children of compulsory school age who needed to receive aid in the form of clothing or books before they could attend school and that when they entered school their advantages were meager in comparison with those of children in other sections. In the peak month, February, 1935, three and one-half million children under sixteen years of age were on rural relief rolls —a vast phalanx of America's future citizenry defeated at the outset of their lives.

The relationship between ignorance and poverty on the one hand and the deaths of young children on the other is well established and needs no elaboration. Ignorance and poverty cause a preventable waste of human life and a vast amount of human suffering that is also preventable.

Both in relief families and in families barely able, by reason of exhaustion of meager personal savings, to keep off relief, children are at a peculiar disadvantage where their medical, dental, and dietary needs are concerned. The recent nationwide health survey showed the greater incidence of sickness among the poor than among relatively well-to-do families.

Whatever differences of opinion there may be as to adults

who are in need, there should be no quarrel with the position that the national interest demands an adequate chance for all of the children. Otherwise the next generation will include a vast number of unfairly handicapped individuals.

To quote again from the findings of the Advisory Committee on Education: "If, for a long period, each succeeding generation is drawn in large numbers from those areas in which economic conditions are poorest, if the population of the Nation continues to be recruited largely from economically underprivileged groups, and if the inability of the depressed economic areas and groups to provide proper education for their children is not corrected by aid from areas and groups more prosperous, the effect on American civilization and on representative political institutions may be disastrous." [8]

---

[8] *Op. cit.*, p. 30.

CHAPTER SEVEN

LANDLESS AND LOW INCOME

FAMILIES

THE TILLERS of the soil in the United States participate less and less in the income from farming. To a smaller and smaller extent do the owners of the land actually produce the crops. On the one hand, when land is operated in large units there is mechanization and the growth of a hired labor class and, on the other hand, increasing land values together with absentee ownership contribute to an increase in tenancy. These landless groups are the submerged workers in agriculture. Their share of the income is low and their status in the community insecure.

In this chapter the social and economic characteristics of the non-landowners in agriculture are discussed. Their relationship to the relief problem is treated in Chapter VIII, "Farmers on Relief."

The ownership of land has become progressively more difficult for a number of reasons. As the population increases, it causes the available supply of land to diminish. Owners die and their heirs in the city prefer to rent rather than to sell. A farmer with two sons and a small farm is usually succeeded by one of the sons, who buys out the

Model of Plantation—Air View

Displaced Tenants

other, leaving him to locate elsewhere. Often, however, the father is not ready to retire when the older son matures, and the son must seek employment elsewhere. The result is that by the time he inherits the land the son is established in some other occupation and rents the farm to a tenant.

Increasing land values and costs of machinery make it more and more difficult for the small farmer to get started. The advantaged classes in agriculture are those which can acquire control of the land and the necessary equipment. The disadvantaged are the landless. The largest cotton agricultural adjustment benefit check went to an English-owned corporation, which profited from the labor of hundreds of low income tenants. The majority of the irrigated acres of Arizona are owned by a few holders who comb the Southwest each fall for laborers to gather their crops at low wages. The intensive orchard and truck economy of Southern California is based on extensive land and capital outlays which can be used for the exploitation of cheap labor.

Formerly the agricultural ladder was the country boy's way to success. He started as a laborer, accumulated enough capital to become a tenant, and then climbed the next rung to ownership. Of course, all did not move up regularly. There were failures as well as successes but, as long as agriculture was expanding, the net increases in the higher classes were steady. As long as all classes—laborers, tenants, and owners—were increasing it was evident that there was some progress up the ladder. The agricultural scene began to change about 1910, however. Tenancy stopped increasing at the expense of the farm labor group and began taking in recruits also from the ranks of unsuccessful owners. Likewise, tenants who failed frequently reverted to the status of laborer, so that the proportion of those on the bottom to those on the top rungs of the ladder grew larger. In periods of depression, as owners and tenants lost their capital, this movement downward was accelerated.

FARM LABORERS

At the bottom of the agricultural scale are the farm laborers. There are three distinct classes in the farm labor group—the home farm laborer, the hired man, and the migratory laborer.

Home farm labor is largely unremunerative, usually taking the form of an exchange of services for board. It is generally performed by a maturing member of the farm family who gains his first agricultural experience in this way. From 1910 to 1930 the trend was toward a smaller number of home farm laborers but from 1930 to 1935 there was a rapid increase as the unwanted labor backed up at home. The decrease from 1910 to 1930 was due partly to the gradual withdrawal of girls from such work and partly to the tendency of boys to remain longer in school. In one sense this category can hardly be counted as part of the permanent agricultural group since its members are really waiting to secure farms of their own or to enter nonagricultural industries.

Formerly the hired man was a young fellow on his way up the agricultural ladder, often the son from a neighboring family. He lived practically as a member of the family of his employer and frequently married his employer's daughter. Today he is less frequently of the same social class and seldom has this favored status.

Hired men vary considerably in the steadiness of their employment. Some shift from farm to sawmill or to public road work and back. Some even drift into the village for short jobs, but they continue to regard themselves as farm laborers. Some, such as plantation laborers in the South, are hired more or less for the year. Others seldom work outside of agriculture, but their employment is chiefly during the peak season.

The development of large-scale production of crops of a highly seasonal nature, requiring extra labor at harvest time, has brought into existence a class of farm labor which is completely nomadic. The casual nature of this employment and the brief duration of each job often force the laborer to cover hundreds, even thousands, of miles within the course of a year. On the other hand, the recurrence of work at regular seasons shortens and gives regularity to his itinerary. Migratory workers in agriculture are, of course, idle during the winter season. Their off-season averages thirteen weeks.[1] The duration of each of their jobs is so short that no permanency is possible. Their families have little or no institutional or community connection. Their children grow up with little discipline and less schooling, and the living conditions in some of their camps are haphazard, unsanitary, and far below accepted standards in general.

The cessation of cityward migration during the depression and the drought caused a marked acceleration of the movement within agriculture. Arizona, California, New Mexico, Oregon, and Washington, and other areas which are widely known havens of migrant laborers were flooded with former farmers of the drought and poor land sections. Many devices were resorted to in an attempt to turn them back at the border. From relief funds they were offered

---

[1] John N. Webb, *The Migratory-Casual Worker*, Research Monograph vii, Works Progress Administration, Division of Social Research (Washington, 1937), p. 113.

payment of their expenses for the return trip home. They were discouraged by every available means. But still they came.

Much of this movement was aimless and temporary and resulted in no real improvement in the economic condition of the migrant. It was largely the result of his feeling that he could hardly be worse off than he was and might through some miracle improve his lot.

The median net earnings (after expenses of travel and subsistence were deducted) of agricultural casual workers studied by the Works Progress Administration [2] were $110 in 1933 for twenty-three weeks' employment and $124 in 1934 for twenty-two weeks' employment, less than half the earnings of migratory workers in industry.

The 1930 census recorded more than two million seven hundred thousand persons as wage workers in agriculture. These included all the gradations of agricultural labor except unpaid work on the home farm. While the laborers were predominantly men and boys, more than one hundred and seventy thousand of them were women and girls. Most of the female workers were in the South with Negroes predominating.

A recent study by the Bureau of Agricultural Economics has covered all types of farm laborers in a variety of type-of-farming areas. In the northern counties surveyed, from one half to three fourths of the laborers were under thirty years of age, but in the other areas older men predominated. One third of all the men were forty years of age and over.[3]

---

[2] *Ibid.*, p. 70.
[3] Tom Vasey and Josiah C. Folsom, "Farm Laborers: Their Economic and Social Status," *The Agricultural Situation* (U. S. Dept. of Agriculture, Bureau of Agricultural Economics, Washington, Oct. 1, 1937), pp. 14–15.

In these age figures lies the real crux of the farm labor problem.

A youth who starts out as a farm laborer can no longer look forward to success unless he expects to escape from this status in his young manhood. The chances are increasingly strong that he will never be able to rise to the ownership level after middle age. Nor is there much hope of bettering himself within the farm labor group. His income is uniformly low and, where perquisites are received in the form of board, lodging, house rent, etc., their value still does not bring the average income up to an acceptable standard.

The employment problems inherent in the farm labor situation were intensified as a result of depression factors. When farm owners were forced on relief in large numbers, all laborers who might have secured employment from them under favorable agricultural conditions were naturally left adrift and frequently became relief beneficiaries themselves.[4] In other cases farmers were able to carry on by curtailing their usual expenses for farm labor, and in some areas the old practice was revived of exchanging labor between owners' families rather than of hiring it. In the severe drought areas harvest labor was not needed because there were no crops to harvest.

Besides the types of farm laborers discussed in this chapter there is yet another depressed class in rural areas which cannot be as readily pigeonholed. This group has no permanent occupational tie-up with agriculture, manufacturing, or trade, but constantly shifts from one to another, normally performing only unskilled work.

The experiences of John Pierce, a young married man of thirty, who lived in an Iowa county seat are in point. After

---

[4] See Chap. VIII.

cornhusking on a farm in the county he was offered a job for the winter on the same farm, but, because the shack in which his wife and he lived was very dilapidated and hardly habitable in cold weather, they went to town. When corn-husking wages were exhausted, they applied for relief, but, because their legal residence was in South Dakota, only emergency assistance was given. Pierce had been engaged in farm work and section labor on the railroad in South Dakota for several years. Jobs became scarce, however, and in the summer of 1937 he made the trip to Iowa with his wife in search of work. In August he registered with the local United States Employment Service. Although he was anxious to work, he had no prospect of employment until spring.

A recent study of migratory-casual laborers reveals many similar histories of wanderers who shift from odd jobs in agriculture to odd jobs in industry and vice versa. Both the number of these drifting unlabeled workers and the rapidity with which they shift from job to job increase markedly with the growth of unemployment and partial employment.

TENANTS

Today almost three million farmers, more than two fifths of all those in the United States, do not own any of the land they operate. Not only has the trend toward tenancy reached alarming proportions but from all indications it may be expected to continue unless positive action is taken to arrest it. The increase in tenancy has been especially rapid during the past twenty years. This has been particularly true of the increase in the share croppers of the South, the lowest class of tenants.

Not all of these tenants can be placed in the disadvantaged class. As a steppingstone for young men on their way into

ownership, tenancy is often a necessary status. This is indicated by the fact that in 1930 nearly one fifth of all tenant
farmers were brothers, children, or grandchildren of their
landlords. In such cases it is evident that tenancy is a form
of family adjustment looking toward ownership and operation of the land and that the tenant has a fair chance eventually to acquire an equity in the property. Tenants related
to their landlords are proportionately numerous in New
England and the Middle West and relatively infrequent in
the South and the drier sections of the Plains Area.

Again, tenants who rent for cash and who have the capital to supply their own work stock, equipment, feed, and
seed stand relatively near the status of owners since their
share of what they produce is reduced only by a fixed rental.
In such cases, however, the leasing arrangement is often not
conducive to the maintenance of the property or the conservation of the fertility of the soil. Cash-rented farms are
rather sparsely distributed since share renting is generally
preferred. However, there are everywhere some farms
that are difficult to rent satisfactorily on a share basis and
some landlords who prefer to rent on a cash basis. Center-
ing in Iowa is a section where many highly desirable farms
are rented for cash to a highly responsible class of tenants.
By contrast many of the farms of Alabama rented in 1930
on a cash basis were small, undesirable farms rented to tenants who commonly had to have the loan or rental of work
animals and advances on which to live while making their
crops. The downward trend of prices of farm products
from the World War to the depths of the depression caused
heavy losses to cash tenants.

Deducting the tenants related to owners and the independent renters, there still remain over half the tenants who
are a distinctly disadvantaged class. The problems of these

groups have been so urgent and they have received so much attention that a special commission has recently prepared a detailed report [5] for the president, and special legislation [6] has been enacted as the beginning of an attempt to solve it.

The proportion of farm operators who are tenants varies considerably from one type-of-farming area to another, but, in general, areas of cash-crop production have especially high tenancy ratios. For example, two thirds of all farmers in the Cotton Belt and almost one half of all farmers in the Corn Belt are tenants. Together these two areas contain over one half of all tenant farmers in the United States. While tenancy has been largely associated with the South, and does reach its most alarming proportions there, it occurs in extremely high ratios in certain sections of many states. In various limited areas of the Midwest, for example, three fifths or more of all farm operators are tenants.[7]

Between 1930 and 1935 tenancy increased most rapidly in the Midwest. It is in the South, however, that it has attracted the greatest attention because of the abject poverty and precarious position of the cotton share croppers. There are about three quarters of a million croppers (half-share tenants) in the South, very few of whom are secure in their means of livelihood. In addition, there are about half as many other share tenants, only slightly better off than croppers. Originally the share tenants of the South were practically all Negroes, but pressure of population and the difficulties of attaining land ownership have created a white tenant class, which is now in the majority.

It is the essence of the share-crop relationship that the

---

[5] National Resources Committee, *Report of the President's Committee on Farm Tenancy* (Washington, 1937).

[6] Public—No. 210—75th Congress, 1st Sess., H.R. 7562.

[7] *Report of the President's Committee on Farm Tenancy.*

cropper furnishes only his labor and the landlord furnishes land, house, animals, and equipment, and advances money for making the crop and, in most instances, for the subsistence of the cropper family during the time when the crop is growing. In return each party to the relationship gets half of the gross proceeds from the sale of the crop, with the proviso that the cropper's half is subject to deductions for his half of the expenses and for subsistence advances. He is thus totally dependent on the landowner for food, shelter, and means of production. His farming operations are laid out for him, his living conditions are what the plantation may afford, and his budget is strictly managed. He is as truly a dependent as was the villein of the Middle Ages.

Since diversified crops are difficult to market, and hence to share, the share-tenant system rests on money-crop production. In the South this means cotton or tobacco. Home-use production is at a discount since the landlord's share depends largely on the money crop. On the other hand, tenants who have the opportunity and energy to raise food crops and livestock enjoy a higher income than those concentrating entirely on cotton.

The South's agricultural finances are perpetually a year behind. The tenant's profit and home-grown food seldom last through the winter, and he must borrow at the beginning of each crop season to produce his crop and to feed his family. Often these loans are passed on by the landlord to the merchant or to the bank. Both tenant and landlord pay high rates for this credit since the only security for it is a precarious crop. Landlords pay as high as 16 per cent and tenants up to 40 per cent in interest. Thus the cotton year starts with a millstone of debt.

Total family incomes in a good year (1934 with a fair

cotton crop at twelve cents a pound) averaged on the efficient plantations $312 for croppers and $417 for other share tenants. This included food raised and consumed by the family. Omitting the cost of such food and deducting advances which had to be repaid, there was left for the average cropper a net cash return of $122. In years of bumper crops the resulting price is so low that the cropper often finds himself worse off than he is with a short crop. The 18,000,000 bale crop of 1937 so reduced the price that it is probable that the average cropper did not have more than $75 in net cash at the end of the year and the lowest fourth either came out in debt or did not have enough to replace the overalls and brogan shoes worn out in working the crop.

Living standards as expressed in the miserable shacks that croppers and other share tenants occupy, the shoddy clothing they wear, and the inadequate diet they consume are indefensible. Here are over a million families who cannot in any real sense be considered a part of the American market. They live in a climate which will produce an amazing variety of sustenance. Yet they can barely exist in good years and know hunger in poor years.

The crux of the tenant problem has recently been concisely summed up by W. W. Alexander as follows:

"Most of the tenants in this country hold the farms they operate on a one year contract. They have no assurance from one year to another that their lease will be renewed when it expires. Hence, they have little opportunity and no incentive to follow a system of soil-building crop rotations; to accumulate livestock, and seed the necessary pasture and hay land; or to exercise the myriad of detailed practices which represent continuous managerial effort toward maximizing the return of the total farm unit. Capital must be kept in a movable form. Crops that can be harvested and sold within a year are desirable, if not necessary. Operating plans must be for short periods and subject to complete abandonment or quick change. As a consequence, the total efficiency of our agricultural plant is greatly reduced, and, at the same time, some of our best land resources are being more rapidly depleted than is necessary or desirable . . .

"Decreased aggregate efficiency and depletion of resources are not, however, the only consequences of our system of tenancy. We have a fairly large body of evidence which indicates that tenants do not participate in community activities to the extent that owner-operators do, and that a high percentage of farm tenancy is inimical to the development of churches, schools, libraries, cooperatives, and similar organizations. When we realize: (1st) that about one-third of our tenants move at the end of every year; (2nd) that the tenant's moving period is often about the middle of the school year, with the consequence that many children have to transfer from one school to another; and (3rd) that most tenants have no assurance that they will be within a given community for more than one year at a time, it is easy to understand why tenancy tends to pauperize the social life of our rural communities." [8]

There is a prejudice in America against the term "peasant." Yet if we accept this word in the European sense as describing a small farm operator with a limited but reasonably secure cash income and with a relatively adequate diet of home-grown food, then we must admit that the levels of living of the majority of tenants and farm laborers do not compare any too favorably with the deprecated peasant.

---

[8] "Farm Tenancy," pp. 6–7, paper read at National Planning Conference, Detroit, Mich., June 3, 1937.

THE AGRICULTURAL FRINGE

Hundreds of thousands of farm families have never attempted to make their full living from the land, and others who make practically their whole living from the farm consume a large proportion of the crops they produce. The characteristics of the so-called part-time farmers and those of the subsistence farmers can conveniently be considered together since there is an extensive overlap between the two groups as defined by the census. It is probable that farmers raising very small commercial crops seek a considerable proportion of their cash income from off-the-farm employment. Conversely, it is apparent from a number of part-time farming studies that most part-time farmers produce largely for home use and only incidentally for the commercial market.

It has been pointed out that 90 per cent of commercial agricultural production comes from about half of the farms and that only about 10 per cent of the marketed products is produced on the other half. That is to say, nearly 3,000,-000 farms having a gross production of less than $1,000 per farm contribute little more than 10 per cent of the marketed products and about 42 per cent of the home-use products. It is within this group of 3,000,000 low income farmers that the vast majority of both the subsistence and the part-time farmers fall. The largest additional class of low income farmers in the category of those earning less than $1,000 is the cotton croppers.

The areas in which these low income families concentrate indicate the centers of part-time and subsistence farming. Areas with the largest proportions of their farms in the hands of this low income group are New England, the cut-over area around the Great Lakes, Tidewater Virginia,

large sections of Florida, the Appalachian Highlands, the
larger part of the old Cotton Belt, the irrigated land of Arizona and New Mexico, and some of the valleys along the
Pacific Coast. With the exception of the Cotton Belt these
are subsistence and part-time farming areas, though there is
a scattering of low income subsistence groups over wide
areas of the land.

Under the census definition any unit to be classed as a
farm must consist of three or more acres or must have agricultural products valued at $250 or more. In defining "farm
types" a self-sufficing farm in 1930 was specified as one
from which more of the products were consumed on the
farm than were sold. Nearly 500,000 farms fitted this definition. A part-time farm was defined as one whose operator
worked 150 days or more for wages off the farm; that is,
the operator must have spent nearly half of his working time
in off-the-farm activity. Also, all farms producing more
than $750 were excluded. About 340,000 farms fell in this
category. On the other hand some 2,000,000 farmers did
some work other than farming. Of these, 29 per cent
worked at nonfarm jobs 1 to 24 days; 17 per cent, 25 to 49
days; 26 per cent, 50 to 149 days; and 28 per cent, 150 days
and over. In other words, if the part-time farmers had been
defined as operators working for outside pay 50 days instead
of 150 days and if farms producing more than $750 had
been included, the number would have risen from 340,000
to over 1,000,000, or one sixth of the nation's farmers who
earn part of their income off the farm.

Thus the census definition of part-time farming greatly
underestimates the number who, to some degree, combine
wage employment with cultivation of the land. In addition there are fully as many combining industrial with agricultural employment who operate between one-half and

three acres as there are those who operate three acres or more.

The income of subsistence farmers is usually low but may run to substantial amounts if crops are supplemented by livestock and domestic animals. More than half the subsistence farms so classified by the census of 1930 had gross incomes of four hundred dollars or less. It must be remembered, however, that these incomes are calculated on the basis of farm prices and that if the commodities consumed had to be purchased at retail prices they would cost considerably more.

A study of the Negro farmers of St. Helena Island [9] disclosed the various types of farming-industrial combinations. The families on the island were divided into three groups: those deriving their major income from farming, those with income about equally divided between farming and wage earning, and those whose wages overbalanced farm income. Few families were found on the island who depended entirely either on wage earning or on farming; nearly every family received some income from both sources.

"The most prosperous of the groups on the Island is the one whose major emphasis is on farming. Their average income is $608 [in 1928], of which $418 [$226 in wages and $192 in crop sales] is in cash. Their larger earnings are not so much attributable to superiority in farming as to their greater energy. The same enterprise which makes them successful in farming drives them, at off times, to tend store, to do carpentering, and in various other ways earn outside money. The average wage for the whole Island is only $212 and these successful families average $226 in wages.

---

[9] T. J. Woofter, Jr., *Black Yeomanry* (New York, Henry Holt & Co., 1930).

Thus, in addition to conducting the most successful farm operations, these men and their families are above the average in wage-earning capacity. But they never neglect the farm. They are always ready to drop other work when farm duties are pressing.

"The group which mixes farming and wage-earning averages about $335 per year, of which about half is from wages and half from the farm. Both in agricultural production and wage-earning these are considerably below the more energetic group.

"The group which depends largely upon wage-earning includes a few carpenters, drivers, porters and many laborers in the oyster canneries. The labor in oyster canneries, of which there are two on St. Helena and one on Ladies Island, is on the piece work basis, men receiving 15 to 25 cents per bushel for gathering the oysters and women 10 cents per can for shucking and putting them up. This group averages in total family income $480, of which $317 is in wages and $163 in produce and use of the owned home." [10]

In a study of the Appalachian Highlands it was pointed out that in 1930 the self-sufficing farms had an average gross income of $464, of which only $141 was from products sold while $323 was from home-use products. For all types of farmers in the whole region the gross farm income averaged $897 or nearly twice that of the self-sufficing farmers. Of this $897 total, $305 came from products for home use and $592 from products sold or traded. Thus, the farming of the region as a whole was on a one-third home-use basis.

As to the mixture of part-time and subsistence farming in parts of the area the report states: "For example, in a farm business and family income study of 203 families living on

---

[10] *Ibid.*, pp. 119–20.

farms in Laurel County, Ky., only 22 families depended entirely on the farm for their living in 1927. Eighty-six of the families had incomes from other sources amounting to less than $200 per family but 48 families had other incomes ranging from $200 to $400, and 47 families had incomes from other sources amounting to $400 or more." [11]

The investment required for modest part-time farming operations is not large. A recent study of part-time farmers in the Southeast [12] revealed that their investment with a few exceptions was little more than that required for housing. Most of them had less than five acres, many less than two acres, and the outlay for equipment, seeds, and fertilizer was not large.

This survey stated: "The value of products consumed by typical part-time farmers during the year ranged from about $70 by part-time farmers who had only a garden to about $400 by those with a garden, a cow, several hogs, and a small flock of poultry. Since the majority of the part-time farmers surveyed made less than $500 a year at their principal off-the-farm employment, the farm's contribution to family living was an important one.

"Although most of the part-time farmers kept a cow, a hog or two, and a flock of chickens, a vegetable garden was the activity that was most general. On half of the farms, gardens produced three or more summer vegetables for 3, 4, and 5 months. Many of the gardens were only ¼ acre in size. Few of the farmers reported three or more vegetables for as long as 8 months, in spite of the long growing season throughout the Eastern Cotton Belt and the small

[11] *Economic and Social Problems and Conditions of the Southern Appalachians*, Miscellaneous Publication No. 205 (U. S. Dept. of Agriculture, Washington, January, 1935), p. 54.
[12] Allen, *et al., op. cit.*

expense attached to garden production. Most part-time farm families were obviously unfamiliar with winter vegetables, but some garden products, such as sweet and Irish potatoes and corn, were stored by two-thirds of the families, while vegetables were canned by three-fifths of the households, thereby prolonging the period of the garden's usefulness through the winter months." [13]

THE SUM TOTAL

The combination of all these groups of low income and disadvantaged farm classes makes up an imposing proportion of the 10,500,000 people engaged in agriculture. A review of the foregoing pages indicates that a majority of the 2,700,000 wage laborers, at least 1,000,000 tenants and croppers, probably 750,000 subsistence and part-time farmers, and a number of small owners living on submarginal lands, or nearly 5,000,000 farm families are suffering from definite handicaps and living at an income level below the minimum subsistence level in cities as defined in recent budgetary studies.

---

[13] *Ibid.,* p. xxxiv.

CHAPTER EIGHT

FARMERS ON RELIEF

AS THE depression of the early nineteen-thirties took increasing toll, American farmers in all sections of the country began their trek to relief offices, eager for the assistance offered by the federal government in the greatest emergency American agriculture had ever experienced. Farm owners as well as share croppers, other tenants, and laborers sought help. In some few instances, in fertile farming country, or in regions not ravaged by recurrent drought, the farmers' need for relief was of recent origin and could be assuaged by temporary assistance. In many cases, however, economic distress had been accumulating over a period of years, and a remedy for deep-seated causes was called for. Thousands of farmers [1] who had sought assistance and were able to leave the relief rolls after a few months were for one reason or another forced to seek aid again at a later date.

Relief needs were definitely related to security on the

---

[1] For more detailed analyses than are practical here, see Berta Asch and A. R. Mangus, *Farmers on Relief and Rehabilitation*, Research Monograph VIII, Works Progress Administration, Division of Social Research (Washington, 1937); Beck and Forster, *op. cit.*; and T. C. McCormick, *Comparative Study of Rural Relief and Non-Relief Households*, Research Monograph II, Works Progress Administration, Division of Social Research (Washington, 1935).

land. In proportion to their total numbers farm owners contributed the fewest relief cases, farm tenants more, and farm laborers still more. Share croppers were represented on the rolls more heavily than other tenants in those sections where share cropping was prevalent.

It must be remembered that this classification is made on the basis of "usual" occupation or the type of farming which had been engaged in longest during the preceding ten years and does not refer to the employment status of the client at the time of seeking relief. Thus some "farmers" on relief had become detached from the land and had been unsuccessful in finding other means of self-support. This detachment from the land was naturally more common among tenants than among owners.

FARM OWNERS

There were approximately two hundred and twenty-five thousand persons usually employed as farm owners receiving federal emergency relief in February, 1935. At least as many more farm owners had been on relief at some time between that date and May, 1933, when the Federal Emergency Relief Administration got under way, or were compelled to seek help before the end of 1935 when that organization was supplanted by the Works Program.

In comparison with other agricultural groups and with people in nonagricultural occupations, farm owners have had low relief rates. In February, 1935, when the relief load in rural areas was near its peak, only one out of every seventeen farm owners in the United States was on relief, but the proportion varied greatly from one type-of-farming area to another. In the prosperous Hay and Dairy Area and in the Corn Belt relatively few farm owners received public assistance, but in the rural problem areas the numbers were much greater than the national average. In the Lake States Cut-Over Area, for example, one out of every five farm owners was on the general relief rolls in February, 1935, and the proportions ran much higher in some of the counties in that area.

The typical farm owner on relief was living in the open country on his farm. The farm obviously was not producing a living for him but he was still there, farming when and as he could, and seeking supplementary employment off the farm to provide the cash he so badly needed. While the farm owner was still living on his farm in most cases, many farmers were living in villages but were continuing to try active farming. This was particularly true in certain sections of the West. Some had given up farming as hopeless and were seeking other occupations. Others had found it advantageous to be close to the village relief office. Some had lost out through foreclosure and some had retired from active farming either just prior to or during the depression and, having lost the rental from the farm, had been forced to seek assistance.

The average farm owner who sank below the level of independence and was forced to ask for relief was found to have been at a definite disadvantage in comparison with his nonrelief neighbors. It was not that he lacked agricultural experience—the great majority of relief farmers had been farming for a decade or more. One of the chief handicaps was that he owned too small a farm. In some places, such as the Western Cotton and Ranching areas, the farms operated by owners on relief in June, 1935, had less than one third of the acreage of the average farm in the area. If a relief farmer had a relatively large farm, his chances of getting off relief were greatly increased. This is indicated by the fact that during the four-month period, February to

June, 1935, the average size of farms of owners on relief decreased from sixty-six to thirty-eight acres. In other words, those with the largest farms regained self-support. Those with the next largest farms were chosen as rehabilitation clients, and those with the smallest farms remained on relief.

Besides being short of land, the typical farm owner on relief lacked adequate stock and machinery with which to operate and was further handicapped by lack of sufficient livestock. He most frequently gave failure of crops or loss of livestock as the reason for his need of public assistance. Other reasons which contributed importantly to his plight, however, were loss or depletion of his assets as a result of depression conditions, loss of supplementary employment in private industry, decreased earnings, and increased needs of his family.

As an individual, the average farm owner on relief was not so different from his neighbors who had remained self-supporting, or who at any rate had not sought governmental aid. He was just about the age of the average farm owner in the general population, the middle forties. There had been a general tendency for the older farmers to move to the villages, but, as the force of the depression struck them, the age difference between open country and village farmers seeking relief was not marked.

They had families which usually consisted of a wife and three or four children. In half of the cases the farmer himself was the only gainful worker in the family—an extremely important point in considering the chances of the family to make a go of the farm without outside assistance. Contrary to the accepted opinion, a large family is not always an advantage on the farm, particularly while the children are small. This does not mean that the wife and children do no farm work but that only the husband can be counted on for a full day's labor.

Practically all of the farm owners who had remained on the land were continuing their farming operations while on relief. Of those living in villages, however, almost one third had either voluntarily retired or had lost their farms and were entirely unemployed. Owing either to lack of openings or lack of desire or ability to change occupations, very few farm owners were trying other jobs. A handful had kept on working in agriculture as tenants, croppers, or laborers, but practically none had tried a job off the land. Most of those who had left their farms had obviously been forced off by the depression, since they had moved since 1930.

Cases of farm families which, under normal agricultural conditions, would have worked out their problems with a minimum of assistance are common on relief rolls. Illustrative of this is the case of Carl Darrow, his young wife, and three little girls who lived on a small acreage in Iowa and did subsistence farming. The farm furnished enough food for home use during the summer and additional vegetables, eggs, and milk that could be sold. In his spare time Darrow was able to hire out as a farm laborer on neighboring farms. When farm production was cut during the early depression and drought years, Darrow's source of outside employment was destroyed. Lack of food, fuel, and clothing forced this family on relief in December, 1935. Darrow is thrifty, his wife intelligent, and, with the return of normal crop and economic conditions, this family should again become self-supporting.

Excessive debts proved the undoing of many during the first years of the depression of the early nineteen-thirties. The Adams family applied for assistance as early as Febru-

ary, 1933. While crop failure resulting from drought conditions was given as the immediate cause of their need for
help, they were struggling under a heavy burden of debt.
Their second-class farm of 280 acres was valued at only
$1,410 but mortgaged for $3,200. Livestock and machinery
were mortgaged for $700 while feed and hospital bills added
to the indebtedness. Adams was fortunate enough to secure a job as rural mail carrier in May, 1936, by which to
support his wife and three small children. In spite of the
discouragement of continued poor crops and excessive ob-
ligations, he has held on to his farm year after year in the
hope of eventually resuming operations.

While the great majority of the farm families which
applied for emergency relief had never before sought assistance, some of them had been known to local relief
agencies for a long time. Typical of these latter was the
Jones family in a northern Wisconsin county. Both Mr.
and Mrs. Jones were in their late forties and neither had
gone beyond the third grade in school. They moved to
Wisconsin prior to the World War and gradually accumulated eighty acres of rough land. They did little farming
but managed to eke out a poor living by selling wood for
ties and pulp. In 1934 the farm was taken out of cultivation as submarginal, and with governmental help the family
was established on a much better farm. Jones was quickly
discovered not to be a success as a farmer even on good
land, however. A son was working in a lumber camp and
the oldest daughter was teaching school. Neither was willing, nor able, to give much help to the parents and the five
brothers and sisters still at home. Since 1932 Jones or one
of his children has had assistance from no less than six government assistance programs. They received $400 as-
sistance in 1933, almost $800 in 1934, more than $800 in

1935, and $265 in 1936. Chronic relief recipients, it is doubtful if this family will ever be wholly self-sustaining.

FARM TENANTS

Even more tenant families than owner families were dependent on federal emergency relief. In February, 1935, more than two hundred and seventy-five thousand tenant families, or one out of every seven such families in the United States, were receiving public support. The extent of the need of financial help for tenants is symptomatic of the basic unsoundness of the tenancy situation and of the crying need for drastic reform.[2]

With such a high proportion of all tenants on relief in a single month, it is probable that more than one out of every four tenants in the entire country has received relief grants at some time during the depression. In the Dakotas, which were suffering from the aftermath of several successive drought years, more than one half of all tenant farmers were on relief in February, 1935, and, in spite of the favorable crop season in a non-drought year which followed, more than 30 per cent of all tenants were still receiving aid in June. Even in the prosperous Corn Belt, one out of every twenty tenants had failed to achieve self-support by June, 1935.[3]

Some of the tenant farmers on relief had moved away from their farms, but 85 per cent of those who were tenants when the depression started were still trying to make a living at farming in the summer of 1935. One third of the tenants on relief in the Corn Belt had left their farms in the spring of 1935, but it was believed that, in this instance, they had frequently been displaced by the return of retired

---

[2] See Chap. VII.
[3] Asch and Mangus, *op. cit.*, p. 51.

owners to their farms during the depression. In most areas, moving away from farms, however unproductive, would have been futile since villages offered slim chances for earning a living. Very few tenants were able to find a niche for themselves in agriculture as farm owners or even as laborers, so most of the tenants who left the farm were totally unemployed in June, 1935. In fact, one out of every eight tenants on relief and still living in the country had no job of any description.

As in the case of owners, the difficulties of farm tenants on relief in 1935 were not due to inexperience, more than two thirds of them having been farming for at least ten years. Many tenants had been forced on relief because of inability to make a living from worn-out or submarginal land, and even a large number were on relief because their farms were too small for efficient operation even if the land had been good.

On every count the average tenant on relief was handicapped with respect to farm production, having little livestock and often possessing only worn-out machinery. Like farm owners, tenants went on relief primarily as a result of crop failures, loss of livestock, loss of private employment, decreased earnings, and increased needs. The tenants with the larger and better equipped farms were the first to take themselves off relief in the spring of 1935 when agriculture began to give signs of shaking off the effects of drought and depression.

The typical tenant farmer on relief was under forty years of age. Families were large, averaging more than five members. The majority of these family members were small children since, in two out of three families of tenants, the farmer was the only adult male member. With large families dependent upon them and with small and poorly equipped farms, it is little wonder that the heads of such families as those described below had to seek federal assistance.

Cases in which ignorance on the part of the tenant and his wife seems to have been a major factor in the economic distress of the family occur frequently. Families whose heads had received at least a grade school education inevitably weathered the depression of the early thirties better or made more successful use of their opportunities to help themselves than their illiterate or semi-illiterate neighbors.

The relief history of the William Orange family in rural Virginia has been a long one although the head of the household was still comparatively young (forty-five years) and three members of the family were employable in 1937. William Orange has always been a farm tenant, and the insecurity of his tenure is shown by the number of moves the family has made within the county, seldom staying more than two years in one location. This man evidently could not get any further up the agricultural ladder, and his own inability and ignorance of farming methods were the principal reasons for it. Orange completed only the fifth grade in school, and his wife only the third. Eight children, the youngest of whom was four years old, complicated the family's economic situation. In the spring of 1937 they were tenants on a five-acre truck farm. It was considered unlikely, however, that Orange could have made a living on it for his large family, even if he had been a more capable and energetic farmer.

A study of cases of families which have moved down the agricultural ladder from ownership to tenancy reveals the almost insurmountable difficulties which many of them face. Tom Wilson, for example, had once been a successful farmer but because of continuous poor crops and low prices over a period of years he had lost practically everything. The mortgage on his land had been foreclosed and he was forced to rent the acres he had formerly owned. He could get no further credit at any of the stores, and, when he applied for assistance in 1933, he had no means whatsoever of supporting his family. The family was given direct relief to supplement the food produced on their farm. The entire family helped with the farm work, although the wife was in very poor health as a result of years of hard work caring for her home and children while she also worked with her husband in the fields.

As has been repeatedly pointed out, one of the major difficulties associated with tenancy is the insecurity of tenure on the land. The Browns were a typical, migratory tenant family, here today and gone tomorrow. Even the encumbrance of ten children did not restrain Mr. and Mrs. Brown from their peregrinations. During the depression they moved annually, usually trying to do truck gardening in whatever happened to be their temporary location. Since the oldest boy was twenty years of age he could help support the family when work could be had. The relief agency finally settled the family on a three-acre plot in the hope that it would eventually become self-supporting, which seems doubtful, however, as this was obviously the case of a laboring man with a family larger than he could adequately support, even with steady employment.

On the other hand, the Clarks were the kind of farm family which restores the faith of those who are depressed by the stories of incompetent families on relief. They were so obviously capable of successful farming that the Resettlement Administration gave them all the assistance needed and in one season they were back on their feet, illustrating what can be accomplished by selected families.

Their story is a common one, a result of depression factors. After operating a stock farm as share tenants for fifteen years they were evicted because the bank, which held a chattel mortgage on the horses and machinery, was in the process of liquidation. The family moved to town, but jobs were scarce and there were seven mouths to feed. Given help in meeting the old debt and regaining his chattels, Clark was able to rent a fertile one hundred and sixty-acre farm with eighteen good milk cows. In the first year the family not only lived well but also bought several hundred dollars worth of livestock and machinery and repaid the bulk of the Resettlement loan. This family had the energy and initiative to make the most of constructive assistance in overcoming temporary misfortune.

FARM CROPPERS

Farmers who cultivate other people's land for a share of the crop are widely scattered over the country, but they are particularly numerous in the Southern States where they are associated with the cultivation of cotton and tobacco.

Although relief rolls in the Southeast had already been markedly pruned by February, 1935, one out of every twelve share croppers in the Eastern Cotton Area was still receiving federal assistance. About twice as large a proportion of share croppers as of other tenants was on relief in this area.[4] In the early spring landlords "furnish" the croppers who are to cultivate their fields and, probably because relief officials felt that work was available, the proportion of share croppers on relief in the Southeast declined to only one in twenty-seven by June. Another factor which helped to decrease the share-cropper relief load was the extension of the rural rehabilitation program which

---

[4] *Ibid.*

provided croppers with the essential goods for a new farming season.[5]

Share croppers, on the average, were between thirty-five and forty years of age. About one out of every ten adults in this class on relief in the early part of 1935 was under twenty-five years of age. Because many of them were quite young, their families were smaller than those of the older owners and tenants, with the cropper himself usually the only truly employable member. Households of former croppers often appeared unduly small on the relief records because of the practice known as "splitting" families. Landlords found it to their advantage to furnish supplies for the employable members of cropper households and to leave the care of the aged and disabled to the relief office.

Croppers are a mobile group.[6] They are constantly in search of better land and more satisfactory working conditions, while the landlords in turn are on the lookout for more satisfactory croppers. Most of the share croppers tend to limit their wanderings to a single county, however, as shown by the fact that more than two thirds of all the share croppers on relief in the two cotton areas in June, 1935, had lived in the same county for ten years or more. Most of them had been little better off before the depression than they were when they received relief grants.

Share croppers were far less successful than farm owners and other tenants in retaining employment during the depression years. Most of those on relief continued to live in the country, but little more than half of those who

---

[5] *Ibid.*, Chap. II.
[6] See T. J. Woofter, Jr., *et al.*, *Landlord and Tenant on the Cotton Plantation*, Research Monograph v, Works Progress Administration, Division of Social Research (Washington, 1936).

stayed were actually farming during the 1935 crop season. A few of the remaining croppers had become farm laborers or tenants, but most of them were without any current employment. Those who had moved to villages had had even less luck in finding work.

Even though they were a relatively young group, croppers had a long history of work on the farm. Almost two thirds of them had worked in agriculture for ten years or more since their sixteenth birthday. On the other hand, one out of fourteen reported only one to three years in agriculture. These were chiefly young farmers who were just getting started or older men who had come back to the country after losing their urban jobs.

The size of acreage cultivated had practically nothing to do with a share cropper's need for relief. A share cropper's acreage is determined by the amount one man can cultivate, and that remains relatively constant. Share croppers who went on relief usually had less fertile farms than those of their nonrelief neighbors, however; they received inadequate support from their landlords, and they were, on the whole, the least competent.

As would be expected, croppers, whether on or off relief, had very little livestock. Half of the cropper families had no cows on their farms. More than two out of five even lacked the ubiquitous pig.[7]

The same general causes which brought farm owners and other tenants on relief were operative in the case of share croppers although loss of employment loomed somewhat larger as many croppers were unable to find farms.

The average amount of monthly relief given to share croppers was pitifully small, amounting to nine dollars per household in June, 1935, or about two dollars per member.

[7] McCormick, *op. cit.*, pp. 45–50, 98–99.

However, croppers received about the same amount of relief as other tenants in the South. All grants were low, re-
flecting the prevailing standard of living. The nine dollars
in cash relief given to croppers was more money than many
of them had ever had to spend in a given month, except for
the fleeting period after annual settlement with the landlord in the fall.

The following case histories, selected at random, indicate
the almost unbelievable destitution of many Southern share
croppers.

The Alexanders were a young share-cropper family
consisting of husband, wife, and three small children.
Both adults had completed grade school. Alexander had
farmed all his life. Since the family had no assets, they had
no borrowing power, and their credit was limited to a
three-dollar grocery bill. When the family first sought relief in 1934, they planned to share crop five acres. Until
the crop matured, they had no source of food except the
charity of neighbors. The one-room log house and its
inmates alike were extremely dirty. Alexander could perform normal work and still have plenty of time for making
his small crop, but he had no opportunity for securing
work off the farm. Apparently doomed to stay on one
federal program after another, he was given the job of
night watchman at the relief office.

The number of relief families consisting of a woman with
dependent children has been particularly large in the South.
Illustrative of this type of household was that of Sally
Mann, a destitute widow with two children at home. The
oldest, a boy fifteen years of age, had to stop school after
completing the first grade to help make the living. The
three lived in a two-room shack with a dirt floor and had
a ten-acre farm to work on a share-cropping arrangement.

The family was willing to work, but they had nothing
with which to work. They went on direct relief in November, 1933, and have continued to receive federal assistance ever since. If the son can eventually secure full-
time employment, he may be able to support the family,
aided by the earnings of his mother, who takes in washing
when she can get it, and his sister, who at thirteen is already
doing her share of the farm work.

When subnormality is added to the other factors de-
termining the need for public assistance, there is practically
no hope of establishing a family, such as the following, on
a self-sustaining basis. Gregory, his wife, and three small
children live in almost unbelievable squalor in a ram-
shackle house of three small rooms. He is sixty years of
age but his wife, representing his second venture in matri-
mony, is only thirty-one. Gregory completed the third
grade in school but his wife, who is obviously feeble-
minded, was incapable of receiving formal education.
Gregory himself is indolent and incompetent. The family
began receiving relief of one kind or another in 1930 and
has been on public relief at intervals ever since. Gregory
is a share cropper, getting one half of his corn and cotton
crop. His share of the 1936 cotton crop, when most
cotton farmers were prospering, brought sixteen dollars.
He raised enough corn for food only. Two hogs were
butchered and a meager garden supplied vegetables for a
few months. Little can be done to put a case of this type
on a self-supporting level. The wife is incapable of improvement. The husband is growing old and has always
been "no account." If the children survive, at least some
of them will probably be subnormal and have to be supported at public expense. Such hopeless cases are, however, only a small proportion of the total.

FARM LABORERS

Farm laborers belong in a different category from the tenant or owner, as they own none of the means of production. They are, however, similar to the Southern cropper in that each contributes his labor only, the cropper taking his return in part of the crop, the farm laborer taking his in wages, pitiably small though they often are. In addition to his money wage, or in place of it, perquisites, such as board, room, house, etc., may be provided.[8] The farm labor population includes many who work on the home farm for their keep, but this chapter concerns only those who work for hire in agriculture on terms comparable with those accorded labor in nonagriculture.

While the actual proportion of farm laborer families on relief cannot be determined for lack of census data, the rate was undoubtedly high. Almost 150,000 farm laborer families were on relief in June, 1935, but more than 275,-000 such families were dependent on federal support in the preceding February.

Farm laborers and share croppers were the youngest of all agricultural groups. But, at that, over half of the farm laborer heads of families were at least thirty-five years of age. One out of every eight was between fifty-five and sixty-five, and most of these older men had probably been farm laborers all of their lives. To them progress up the agricultural ladder was only a fiction.

The families of farm laborers contained about one person less, on the average, than those of farm operators. They were approximately the same size as families of non-agricultural workers in rural areas (4.5 persons). One of

---

[8] See Chap. VII.

the reasons for the comparatively small size of their families was the younger average age of the farm laborers.

The farm laborer families, like those of the share croppers, did considerable moving about but it was limited largely to their home counties. Two thirds of them had lived in the county in which they were receiving relief for at least ten years. However, one in six had lived in the county of residence less than five years. The greatest mobility was evident in the Western Cotton and Wheat areas, regions of relatively recent settlement. These are also sections where transient labor, which moves on at the end of the season, is employed most frequently.

Farm laborers were in dire straits in 1935 as a result of lack of work due to both drought and depression. Four out of five family heads on relief were without employment of any kind. Only one out of eight had managed to find work at farm labor, while a few had rented farms or had found odd jobs at unskilled labor in the villages.

By and large farm laborers had done little else in their lives. Over half of them had worked on farms for ten years or more since they were sixteen years of age, and only one in ten had had less than four years of experience, but experience at unskilled labor was the only equipment most of them had for making a living in agriculture.

In so far as a large number of workers in a family is an advantage, farm laborers were even more handicapped than farm operators. In three out of four households the farm laborer himself was the only employable member, and usually the family had gone on relief because he had lost his job or had had his earnings cut to the point where he could not provide the necessities of life.

The insecurity of the economic position of this class of worker, even under conditions of normal employment, is indicated by the fact that the average farm laborer was forced to apply for relief only three months after losing his job. Farm owners, on the average, were able to maintain themselves for thirteen months after their farms ceased to be a source of income, and farm tenants for seven months. Although farm laborers had little supplementary employment, and usually a minimum of farm produce, their average monthly relief grant (twelve dollars in June, 1935) was about the same as that of farm operators.

The problem of adequate support from earnings at farm labor is not limited to the relief group. However, typical case histories from this group indicate the types of problems faced by practically all farm laborer families.

John and Edith Bush reached the peak of their prosperity during World War days. Bush alternated between work as a farm laborer and work on the highways during the slack season in agriculture. The family was able to buy a small house and barn in the home village with enough land to make possible some truck farming in addition to the growing of vegetables for home consumption. Bush also bought a truck in which he hauled wheat, potatoes, and other products in season. He had an oil company job on the side until 1929. After that the family of five subsisted on his earnings from trucking and odd jobs which gradually dwindled away. In December, 1934, when the grocery bill had mounted to $345 and the doctor's bill to $150, the family had no alternative but to apply for relief.

Peter Mackintosh, who was born and reared on a farm in a midwestern county, was only thirty-one years of age when he first asked for aid. He had received only a grade school education and was trained for nothing but farm work. His father was one of the early settlers in the county and had prospered. Had the land continued to produce, all of the sons would have been settled on farms by the father with enough money to start farming for themselves. However, the soil was worn out, years of poor crops had depleted the father's resources, and he as well as the sons was forced to seek work as a day laborer. Since 1933 the head of this family had been endeavoring to support his wife and six children by working as a day laborer, his wages ranging from a dollar a day to five dollars during harvest time. The work in this county is all seasonal farm work and after seeding in the spring and harvesting in the fall the farmers employ practically no one. If this family could be located on a good farm, it would become self-supporting. There is no possible chance of the father's being able to support six children on his wages as a farm laborer in the present location, and, if he finds no other work, he will have to be assisted during periods of unemployment until his children are grown and have become self-supporting.

McWhite was employed irregularly as a farm laborer in the summer of 1934. Since his employment was inadequate to support himself and his wife, they were given relief grocery orders as needed. The next year the McWhites moved to a small farm in the hope of becoming self-supporting. They had been renters from 1917 to 1925, and after failing in that capacity McWhite had been employed on various farms. He secured WPA employment early in 1935 and then worked at farm labor during the summer. When that played out, he again sought WPA work. Obviously, if agricultural conditions should pick up to where wage opportunities were more frequent, he should be capable of supporting himself and his wife and might eventually rise on the agricultural ladder.

PART-TIME AND SUBSISTENCE FARMERS

Part-time farming undoubtedly reduces the likelihood of need for relief. Having two strings to their bow the family incomes of part-time farmers are more dependable. It is not possible to prove this hypothesis from existing studies of part-time farmers since by definition a part-time farmer must have worked for wages for a substantial period and such employment always decreases the probability of the need for relief.

A recent study conducted by the Works Progress Administration [9] concluded that within the same communities there was little difference between the proportions of part-time farmers and of full-time industrial workers who were on relief although the indications were that the part-time farmer was likely to be on relief for a shorter period and that the amount of relief needed was likely to be smaller.

Income from the part-time farm is seasonal and complete loss of industrial employment in the winter is likely to be almost as serious for the part-time farmer as for the full-time industrial worker. Also, many industrial workers when unemployed attempt to carry on farm operations without the requisite skill or capital or on unsuitable land. This is evidenced by the fact that large numbers of people on the relief rolls of the Appalachian-Ozark Area and the cut-over area around the Great Lakes were engaged in farming, although their usual occupations were nonagricultural. They had lost their jobs, tried farming, and failed to produce enough to keep off relief. Much of the back-to-the-farm movement during the depression was of this character. Farm increases from 1930 to 1935 were

---

[9] Allen, *et al., op. cit.*

most pronounced in areas around cities and in part-time and subsistence farming areas.

The relationship of subsistence farming per se to relief is not clear. A balanced production could supply many of the food needs of the family. When accompanied by a modest cash income either from limited crop sales or from some outside employment, it should result in a stable budget, not subject to the fluctuations of the market or the failure of any one crop.

Subsistence areas are, however, with the exception of New England, high relief areas. An important element in the situation is indicated by the fact previously stated that subsistence farmers were usually found to have been more or less part-time farmers, so that loss of supplementary employment in mines and forests came as a serious blow to the family budget. Again, since the better lands command higher prices from the commercial farmers, subsistence and part-time farming is usually confined to the poorer and less productive land, much of which should not be in cultivation. Most subsistence farmers are in the very low income brackets. The gross farm incomes of many of them run below four hundred dollars, which means that they have little chance to accumulate reserves. Add to this the fact that cultivation of the land is a side line with many and therefore is approached with ignorance and inexperience. Altogether there is a combination of unfavorable factors here which militates strongly against the success of subsistence farming as now practiced.

The need for relief in the commercial farming areas was greatly reduced by the benefit payments under the Agricultural Adjustment Program. These payments made on the basis of the retirement of land previously planted to commercially marketed crops did not reach the live-at-home farmers to an appreciable extent. The amount of money paid under the various adjustment acts to the farmers of New England, the Lake States Cut-Over Area, and the Appalachian Mountains was comparatively negligible. Relief loads in the Cotton Belt were early reduced by the recovery in the major crop, and relief needs in the Western Cotton and Wheat areas were strongly cushioned from the effects of drought by heavy benefit payments, while the Corn Belt has never been an area of pronounced rural need. Subsistence farmers were, however, left to shift for themselves. If they could not work out their own salvation, there was nothing for it but to go on relief. This partially explains the fact that rural relief in subsistence areas has remained consistently high throughout the depression.

CHAPTER NINE

VILLAGERS ON RELIEF

FARMERS AND farm problems have tended to dominate America's thinking about the relief situation in rural areas. Actually, however, farm cases have constituted only about half of the total rural relief load. Of the heads of rural families who received general relief in February, 1935, nearly one half had had nonagricultural occupations or were village dwellers without an occupation. To the extent to which they live in predominantly agricultural villages the fortunes of this group rise and fall with those of the farm population. If crops are good and prices high, the farmer can buy more supplies for his farm and more necessities and luxuries for his family: more clothes, more dental work, more telephones, more movies, and longer school terms. When farmers fail, agricultural villages stagnate.

Many rural workers, on the other hand, have little to do with farming. They are the ones employed in scattered industries—the miners and lumbermen, the fishermen, and the employees of small factories. Small villages, such as the unincorporated textile villages of the South, dominated by a single manufacturing plant, are familiar sights in many sections of the country. In some regions the factories are on the outskirts of cities. But a worker in such a factory

is distinguished from his urban counterpart by the fact
that he and his family can have a garden, a pig, a cow, and
a few chickens if they so desire; and he, too, is included in
the rural category. He is subject in varying degrees, however, to all the ills of industrial depression that his city
brethren experience. But whether their problems are
temporary, caused by depression factors, or are destined to
be permanent, because they live in villages which have
permanently lost their major industries, the acuteness of the
need in hundreds of villages has become so self-evident
that the term "stranded community" has gained currency.

COLLAPSE OF RURAL INDUSTRIES

Inasmuch as the industrial support of far-flung rural areas
is largely dependent on lumbering and mining, the likelihood of infusing new life into them is directly dependent
upon the prospects of those industries. In both cases the
troubles of the industry are more deep-seated and longstanding than the dislocation which occurred in 1929 and
the following years when all industries felt the effects of
the general depression.

According to reports of the census, the number of bi-
tuminous coal mines decreased from 8,300 in 1919 to 5,600
in 1929, in spite of an increase in total production. In the
same period, wage earners in the industry decreased by
nearly 100,000. Thus, even before 1929 the closing of
low producing mines and the introduction of laborsaving
machinery were eliminating masses of miners. The heaviest reductions occurred in the small, scattered mines around
the fringe of the coal region. Workers in such fields found
it necessary to adjust themselves to both a new occupation
and a new locality or else to shift to agriculture on near-by
lands. Many of them will probably never get back into

coal mining. All through the Appalachian coal valleys grimy, decaying villages are the result. In each village some of the families hang on in the vain hope of resumption of operations and meanwhile lead a squalid existence.

What is true of coal mines is to a lesser extent true of the iron mines which were operating on low profits. Then, too, as oil fields shift, villages are left stranded; and on a smaller scale there is the problem of stranded lead and zinc and copper mining villages.

The problems of lumber villages are somewhat different. They arise from the exhaustion of the forests. When the trees have gone, the industrial resource of the village has gone, and the worker must again follow the sawmill or shift to some other occupation, such as agriculture.

Similar problems arise with the shift of other industries. The trend of the textile industry southward has left stranded textile areas in New England. Whenever a plant which is the sole pay roll source of a small community considers a move, its workers must consider the possibility of unemployment. Since lower labor costs are often a primary consideration and the plant may move a considerable distance, the workers have little opportunity to change to the new locality.

Whether or not it is possible to introduce stabilizing factors into this extremely mobile pattern of American industry is problematical.

EXTENT OF VILLAGE RELIEF

Rural families which do not earn their living from the farm present an even more difficult relief problem than farm operators or farm laborers. Some village populations have been represented on relief rolls in appallingly large proportions. In June, 1935, one in every eight village families, exclusive of nonagricultural families in the open country, was subsisting on federal relief funds.

There was marked variation from one part of the country to another, however. In the prosperous Hay and Dairy Area in the Northeastern States, only one out of thirteen village families was on relief rolls in June, 1935. In the Lake States Cut-Over Area, one out of every four families was receiving federal assistance. High as this proportion was, families in villages were not as dependent on relief as those in the open country in this area of wasted forests. Almost as serious a relief situation was indicated in villages of the Dakotas, where, by reason of heavy incidence of drought distress in centers of population which depended upon agriculture for their prosperity, one out of five village families in the Spring Wheat Area had to fall back on federal funds.

The usual occupations of the heads of village households who have come on relief show them to be a group with few skills and scant opportunity for the accumulation of financial reserves even in normal times. About one fourth of the village heads of households who were actually working or looking for work reported themselves as usually engaged in agriculture, but the majority of such agricultural workers were farm laborers and therefore faced with all the insecurity incident to this type of employment. About two out of five village heads of households were unskilled industrial laborers. Together with farm laborers this group made up more than half of the employable relief load in villages. About one in five was a skilled or semiskilled workman while white-collar workers were far less numerous.

The reasons given by villagers on relief for having sought public assistance present a cross section of the meaning of the depression to the families caught between the two overwhelming forces of industrial and agricultural decline. Loss of employment and loss of assets were the chief causes of village distress in all sections of the country —the cause of the destitution back of cases that had been on relief in earlier years as well as of those coming on relief for the first time in the summer and fall of 1935. Over half of the village workers with a work history who were accepted for relief from July through October, 1935, had lost their jobs in private industry, although this was a period of general business recovery. Many who had secured temporary work and who had been able to leave the relief rolls for a short time were again asking for public assistance during this period.

Not only did loss of a job or decreased earnings send these village families on relief but also they were compelled to apply soon after losing employment. After long years of depression they had no savings accounts, no salable assets, and no credit to tide them over several months of unemployment. The length of time a village family could remain economically independent after the head of the household had lost his usual job, however, varied considerably from one type of occupation to another. Unskilled workers went on relief, on the average, only three months after they lost their jobs since they had neither reserves on which to live nor assets against which they could borrow. Even skilled workers remained off relief only eight months. Professional workers, those at the top of the nonagricultural economic ladder, were able to get along for slightly over a year.

Another important factor in the village relief situation was the large proportion of households with women as their economic heads. Ten per cent of the households on relief in June, 1935, were fatherless households where the mother was the economic head, and an additional 7 per cent of the cases consisted of women living alone or women in households with other persons. Relief figures revealed the marked tendency of unattached women—widows, divorcees, and spinsters—to concentrate in villages.

More than two thirds of the village relief households consisted of husband and wife, or husband, wife, and children, but one out of every twelve or thirteen was a man living alone. Men on relief living alone were numerous in the North woods, where many of the lumberjacks have no family connections, although unattached men formed a part of the relief load everywhere.

The presence of many young village boys loafing in beer parlors and poolrooms has focused attention upon them and caused them to be regarded as a particular problem in rural areas. Although idleness and unemployment are also common among young people living in the open country, their plight has not been so noticeable as that of village youth.[1]

Large numbers of village households were on relief for the simple reason that they contained no person who could take a job in private industry, even if a job became available. In comparison with open country households, fewer of the members of village households other than family heads in the productive age groups were seeking work. Moreover, aged persons who were no longer in the labor market were more numerous in the villages than in the open country, and many of these were women.

Jobs—even inadequate ones—were hard to find in June, 1935, and three out of four heads of village relief house-

---

[1] Melvin, *op. cit.*

holds usually engaged in nonagriculture had no work at all. Only one out of every ten nonagricultural relief heads of families who had had predepression jobs in work other than farming had managed to retain employment in his usual field. A few who had lost their usual jobs had tried their luck at farming but, whether they had professional training or were unskilled day laborers, their story of unemployment was much the same.

The extent to which part-time farming ventures will serve as bulwarks against periods of unemployment or underemployment is far from satisfactorily settled. If part-time farming is to be a sort of backlog to carry the family through economic crises, nonagricultural rural workers on relief have few of the requisites. Only one out of seven had a cow. The same small proportion reported a pig or two. Only three out of five had a small flock of chickens —scarcely large enough to give a meager supply of eggs and an occasional fowl for the pot.[2] Yet there are few villages where such livestock would be prohibited by reason of lack of space. Like their farm neighbors, villagers on relief had only a minimum of this world's goods of any kind.

TYPES OF RELIEF CASES

The following selected case histories illustrate the variety of nonagricultural relief problems in rural areas.

Lack of employment opportunities for unskilled labor was entirely responsible for the distress of Jess Martin and his family. He had a steady job as a factory hand in a flooring plant until 1931 when the plant burned. Since then his employment has been decidedly miscellaneous. He has taken whatever work he could get, regardless of

[2] McCormick, *op. cit.*, p. 47.

A Mining Village

Man-made Destitution

its duration. Many times his employment has been insufficient to support his family which consists of a wife and three children. Since less than two acres of his land are fit for agriculture, relief has become necessary. For most of 1934 and 1935 the family received intermittent aid: direct cash relief, work relief, and surplus commodities. Before the Emergency Relief Administration came into existence, the family was aided by the Red Cross, by the Associated Charities, and by a private individual. Yet with improved business and industrial conditions, this family and many others like it will present no relief problem.

The transference of coal mining operations to another locality left Sam Harding stranded in an almost deserted village. The surrounding country was too poor and rocky for farming, and, since nearly all of the timber had been cut, little work remained. A few men in the village obtained intermittent work in coal mines or on farms some distance away. The majority eked out a bare existence for their families from relief, miserable gardens, and occasional hunting.

Sam Harding has been having a desperate struggle to get along since the mines closed twelve years ago. He is now fifty-five years old and has always been a miner. He did unskilled work and earned only fifteen dollars a week even in good times. The two boys, sixteen and seventeen years of age, were classified as employable by the local agency. Neither has held a regular job, but both have had odd jobs in various coal mines in the county. Mrs. Harding and a girl thirteen years of age were the other members of the family. Last year the Hardings cultivated a small garden. The soil was poor, however, and produced very little.

Relief has been the only recourse for these people. The head of the family is now too old to compete for a job in coal mining, even if local activities should be resumed. He knows little of farming which is the only industry of importance in the county, and he lacks money to move from his present residence to seek other employment.

One federal agency after another had given aid to William Curtis, a Negro laborer, his wife, and fifteen children. Curtis could not remember his work history prior to 1933 except that he had held odd jobs, always for short periods. His meager earnings had frequently been supplemented by relief allotted by the township trustees. He was first given federal aid during the winter of 1933–34. Then in the spring the family was supplied with food, clothing, garden seeds, and one hundred baby chicks. The township trustees lent them a cow. With this assistance they managed to be partially self-supporting the rest of the year. Curtis had work in the coal mines during November and December, but by January, 1935, the family was again in dire need. They lacked clothes, fuel, and food, and relief was their only recourse.

The children, who were all in good health, were in regular stairsteps from one to eighteen years of age. Somehow they all squeezed into a four-room house which contained only the most necessary furniture. It was extremely dirty when visited by the case worker. On account of lack of dishes and kitchen utensils the family ate from the kettle in which the meal was cooked. Curtis boasted three years of schooling and his wife four. The children were apparently going through grammar school although the seven- and eight-year olds had yet to attend school. Obviously the father had more mouths in his family than he could feed except under the most favorable circumstances. Since the small Ohio town in which he lived offered few opportunities for day labor, it seemed that he would continue to need public assistance through either direct or work relief for many years.

Illness, loss of the usual job, and the difficulty of making an immediate adjustment to a new job have been causes of many requests for relief. A good example is the case of Tom Drake who became ill and lost the job in a grocery store on which he, his wife, and his young son were dependent. The family lived in Quarry, a small village with a population of only 144, where work opportunities for white-collar workers were extremely limited. In 1934 the household was given food, fuel, clothing, and medicine to the amount of $80. In 1935 surplus commodities were added to the 1934 allotment. The problem in this case was primarily one of health since Drake could find a job if he were well enough to work. Both Drake and his wife were high school graduates and intelligent.

A similar type of case in another field was that of a skilled diemaker. Sam Erwin made a good living for himself, his wife, and young daughter and son in a small Iowa town. He was employed in automobile manufacturing plants. While diemaking is highly skilled, it is seasonal, offering employment only in the summer months. Though wages were good during the season, it was not possible for him to save a great deal. Consequently, when Erwin became ill and was declared a borderline tubercular case, he had no savings to tide him over. Relief help was intermittent, covering a period of two years from April, 1934, to March, 1936. Medicine, food, fuel, clothing, and surplus commodities were given in addition to work relief.

Investigators reported that this family made a desperate effort to stay off relief. When Erwin was laid off at the automobile plant in the fall, he expected to get a job picking corn in Marshall County, Iowa. He rode through the country for three weeks trying to get a job before giving up. At the present time he is trying to learn a type of the diemaking business that will keep him out-of-doors, as continued work indoors will be very injurious to his health. When last reported on, Erwin had an odd job and the family was temporarily self-supporting.

The country is dotted with towns, villages, and hamlets whose problems have not received the close scrutiny applied to those of the large city and the farm. Some are trading and processing centers for vigorous farm areas, and others are built around sound industries which assure relative security for the population. Others depend on the seasonal and uncertain operations of marginal mines or factories in which employment is at low wages and sporadic. Planning for sound use of human resources will involve gauging the occupational outlook of each hamlet and village and in the more hopeless cases persuading at least part of the people to leave these stagnant pools of underemployment.

CHAPTER TEN

REGIONS OF CHRONIC DISTRESS

EVEN THE casual observer of the situation in rural sections of the United States during the depression years must have been impressed with the variations in economic conditions. In some regions practically all of the usual methods of earning a livelihood were furnishing little or no employment, owing to adverse agricultural conditions or to the closing down of rural industries. In other regions, where agriculture is less subject to climatic and economic vagaries, rural destitution was less serious. The farmsteads in some sections were well-kept and adequate, but in others they were cheerless and dilapidated.

When the Federal Emergency Relief Administration began to receive increasingly insistent demands for assistance outside of cities, a careful study of the underlying causes revealed the fact that large regions are chronically underprivileged. Throughout the depression years these have stood out by reason of intense concentration of rural distress within their borders. The main rural problem areas have been designated as the Eastern Cotton, Western Cotton, Appalachian-Ozark, Lake States Cut-Over, Spring Wheat, and Winter Wheat.[1] In addition to these broad

---

[1] See Beck and Forster, *op. cit.*

regions there are numerous smaller areas in which conditions have been equally as desperate. Each area whether large or small represents a somewhat different combination of handicaps, but all are alike in having at some time contained disproportionately large numbers of people on relief.

In such places hard times were not new to many families. The depression of the early thirties was the culmination of a series of adversities, many of them of long standing. The depression focused the attention of the nation upon these sore spots and, with the stocktaking that accompanied the release of federal funds for general relief, their plight became obvious.

The distress of a few families in a county presents individual problems but no serious social menace. When over thousands of square miles, however, a large proportion of all rural families live so near the ragged edge of destitution that the slightest reverse creates a need for assistance, the situation assumes national proportions. In such sections trade is stagnant, social institutions are scattered and poorly supported, and living is more primitive than we would care to acknowledge as typical of hundreds of thousands of twentieth-century Americans. Furthermore, these areas of low economic opportunities are usually areas with high birth rates, causing continuous movement of maturing youth into more favored sections.

EASTERN COTTON AREA

The Eastern Cotton Area includes those portions of North Carolina, South Carolina, Georgia, Alabama, Mississippi, Louisiana, and Arkansas in which cotton culture is the dominant type of agriculture. The problems of the cotton farmer are not of recent origin. Periods of depressed cotton prices were so frequent from 1910 to 1935 that the poor years outnumbered the good. Before the recent entry of the federal government into the field of production control, it was not difficult to prognosticate the year-to-year fluctuations in the cotton situation. If prices were high one year, cotton farmers expanded their acreage the next. After a year or two of excess production, the surplus forced prices down and acreage was reduced. This in turn raised the price and the cycle started over again.[2]

During the decade and a half beginning in 1910, cotton farmers in the Eastern Cotton States were faced with the destruction wrought by the boll weevil as their farms were progressively laid waste. In 1910 the ravages of the boll weevil were serious in Mississippi. The pest spread annually and by 1921 the whole Eastern Cotton Area was overrun. As a result there are today millions of acres of abandoned farm land in the Southeastern States. Another factor contributing to the abandonment of acreage is the wide distribution of gullied land, barren of its once fertile topsoil.[3] There was actually less acreage in farms in the Southeast in 1930 than in 1860, although improved acreage had increased.

Associated with these factors were tremendously significant changes in farm operation. At the beginning of the Civil War practically all whites engaged in agriculture were owners who either had relatively large holdings cultivated by slaves or who operated family sized farms with occasional hired labor. Between 1860 and 1930, however, the total number of males engaged in agriculture in North

---

[2] For a detailed analysis of the factors associated with cotton culture, see Woofter, *et al.*, *Landlord and Tenant on the Cotton Plantation.*

[3] See *National Resources Board Report, December 1, 1934,* Part II, Section III (Washington, 1934).

Carolina, South Carolina, Georgia, Alabama, Mississippi, Louisiana, and Arkansas increased from slightly over one million to more than two million. While Negro males engaged in farming were increasing only 3 per cent, whites were increasing nearly 300 per cent.[4]

The small landowner and tenant alike in the South are chained to a cotton economy with its wide fluctuations in price, ruinous debt structure, and dependence on world prices for prosperity. The agrarian difficulties are greatly complicated by lack of industrial opportunity within the region sufficient to absorb a large portion of the excess population increase.

In most attempts to reconstruct the economic life of the nation the puzzling question of what is the way out for the Old South eventually becomes a stumbling block. Foreign trade—cotton is one of our chief exports. Race problems—the Old South, until recently, had a monopoly on the complex question of relationships between white and Negro. Tenancy—its most unsatisfactory manifestation is in the South. Population pressure—by far the greatest stream of interregional migration springs from the Southeast. And so on through the whole gamut of knotty questions which confront the nation. Sooner or later the difficulties of the South always complicate any sort of national solution.

As a result of the system, living conditions are often deplorable. In 1934 almost one in four of all houses of white farmers and almost one in three of all houses of Negro farmers in the Eastern Cotton States had no sanitary facilities whatsoever.[5] Food is scant in quantity and poor in

---

[4] Woofter, *et al., Landlord and Tenant on the Cotton Plantation,* p. 12.
[5] Farm Housing Survey by Bureau of Home Economics, U. S. Dept. of Agriculture in co-operation with Civil Works Administration.

A Dust Storm

Farmers at Work

quality, and a diet too largely composed of meal, salt pork, and molasses results in high sickness and death rates. In 1930 the seven Eastern Cotton States had almost two and one-half times as many deaths from pellagra, a dietary disorder, as all the rest of the states in the registration area together.[6] High birth rates continue to add to an already excessive rural population.

This area, with its millions of impoverished rural people, contributed thousands upon thousands of cases to the federal relief rolls in 1933 and 1934. To a considerable proportion of these families the monthly relief grant, which averaged ten dollars in February, 1935, represented a degree of economic security greater than they had ever previously experienced. During the latter part of 1934 and throughout 1935 relief rolls were reduced greatly by the Rehabilitation Program [7] with its emphasis on helping farm families to regain self-support, by the gradual increase in the stringency of rules for the acceptance of relief cases, and by the return of unemployable cases to local relief. Such reductions, however, did not signify a change in the basic situation—chronic destitution of thousands upon thousands of both white and Negro rural families.

WESTERN COTTON AREA

For historical and geographical reasons the Eastern and Western Cotton areas have had differing developments, but major reliance on cotton causes them to be considered as two related parts of one whole. The Western Cotton Area has been generally delimited as including those counties in

---

[6] U. S. Bureau of the Census, *Mortality Statistics, 1930*, Tables 1A and 6.
[7] See "The Rural Rehabilitation Program," *Monthly Report of the Federal Emergency Relief Administration, August 1 Through August 31, 1935*, pp. 14–24.

Texas and Oklahoma in which cotton culture predominates. This area was settled somewhat later than the Eastern Cotton Area and, since the western extension of cotton culture has been a development primarily of the twentieth century, the pattern of plantation ownership common to the eastern section has not been followed. Many of the farmers who pushed westward attempted to produce a livelihood on farms too small for efficient operation. The expansion of mechanized methods of cultivation in this area, which is particularly adapted to large-scale agriculture, has resulted in reduced labor demands in relation to production and has caused too much of that demand to become seasonal in nature.

As in the wheat areas to the north, the large demand and high prices brought about by the World War led to rapid increases in cultivated acreage. Moreover, the fact that the boll weevil was playing havoc with cotton farms to the east gave the cotton farmers west of the Mississippi another impetus toward expansion. But like their neighbors to the east, the cotton farmers of the West also felt the demoralizing effects of periodically reduced prices. These in turn resulted in a downward trend in acreage, but migration of agricultural workers into the area continued. Hence, an excess of farm tenants and laborers, many needed for only short periods, if at all, has proved a particularly acute problem of the area.

In parts of this section rainfall is always a major question.[8] In at least one part of the area cotton failures are reported one year in five.[9] While dry years were one of

---

[8] F. D. Cronin and H. W. Beers, *Areas of Intense Drought Distress, 1930–1936*, Special Report, Works Progress Administration, Division of Social Research (Washington, 1937), pp. 7–11.

[9] Kifer and Stewart, *op. cit.*, Chap. III.

the long-range factors which contributed to the mounting distress of the early years of the depression, the extreme droughts of 1934 and 1936 with their wake of dust storms brought added destitution since farmers lost part or all of their crops.

The Western Cotton Area is further disadvantaged by distance from markets. Ocean-going freight rates make it cheaper to export cotton from Texas than to ship it to the Atlantic Seaboard, which renders this section particularly vulnerable to loss of foreign markets.

Plagued by the same factors that are characteristic of other Southern areas—lack of education, inadequate incomes, excess agricultural population, and general low standards of living—problems of public welfare are acute. According to a recent study of relief in rural sections of Texas, "at least one-third of the families on relief in these areas were largely dependent upon the uncertainties of seasonal labor and odd jobs for a livelihood. Even a regular income from this source would scarcely support a family of several members beyond a bare subsistence. In this respect, unsanitary living conditions, malnutrition, and other evils attendant upon an extremely low-income existence had marked most of this group as potential recipients of relief long before the onset of the depression." [10]

While relief rolls in the Eastern Cotton Area have been crowded with whites and Negroes, Mexicans have constituted an added burden to rolls of the Western Cotton Area. Preponderantly in those underprivileged groups from which relief recipients are drawn most heavily under any

---

[10] C. E. Ullrich, *A Study of Family Heads and Other Members in the Texas Rural and Town Relief Population, October 1935,* Preliminary Report No. 5 (Texas Agricultural Experiment Station, College Station, Tex., Feb. 15, 1937), p. 2.

circumstances, Mexican families have had consistently high relief rates in this area.

APPALACHIAN-OZARK AREA

Perhaps the one rural problem area which was most fully recognized as such long before the depression was the Appalachian-Ozark Area. Scores of writers have made the nation conscious of the poverty and illiteracy, however picturesquely they may be presented, of this area which includes, roughly, the highland regions of West Virginia, Virginia, North Carolina, Tennessee, and Kentucky, together with the Ozark counties of Missouri and Arkansas.

Settled early by self-reliant pioneers from northern and western Europe, the later westward waves of migration passed beyond and left it in a state of comparative isolation in which it remained for decades. Even today its population is almost wholly native white. The early settlers located first in the fertile valleys, and later on the less productive highlands, and since the birth rates have continued to be excessively high, the pressure of population upon the land has been constantly increasing. Originally fertile farms were worn out or subdivided into units too small to provide more than the barest support, and less and less fertile land was subjected to the plow. Denuded of protective vegetation, steep hillsides have been subject to rapid destructive erosion.

With the advent of the railroads and the exploitation of lumber and mineral resources, the area became, of course, less isolated and its economy, therefore, less self-sufficing. While retaining their tiny farms for food production, the mountain workers flocked to the mines and lumber mills which offered opportunity for cash wages.

Eventually, forests were cut over and unprofitable mines

were abandoned, and the onset of the depression revealed a
great group of families once more reduced to trying to eke
out a living from mountain farms.   Here, as in other areas,
part-time or subsistence farming has proved to be inadequate for providing a suitable standard of living when there
are no sources of supplementary cash income available.
Meanwhile the population, which was already taxing the
means of subsistence, has continued to expand during depression years—an expansion that was increased by the
virtual cessation of the flow of young people to urban areas.
There was, indeed, an actual return flow of population to
many rural communities.

In spite of increasing efforts to eradicate illiteracy, the
proportion of the population in the area unable to read and
write remains a national disgrace.   Even with the low
standard of living, relief rates were high throughout the
period of federal relief.   Benefits were low, however, in
comparison with all other areas except the Cotton South,
indicating the depressed living standards of the recipients.

The conditions brought to a focus by the depression have
been concisely summarized as follows: "Lack of economic
opportunities [in the southern Appalachians] is associated
with lack of roads. Lack of roads results in economic and
cultural isolation of families and communities. Poverty
and isolation tend to lower the physical, mental, and moral
development and to undermine the economic efficiency of
the population. Inadequate medical attention, poor diet,
ignorance of hygiene, inadequacies of housing, and similar
factors contribute to a high death rate and tend to undermine the economic efficiency of the population." [11]

---

[11] *Economic and Social Problems and Conditions of the Southern
Appalachians*, Miscellaneous Publication No. 205 (U. S. Dept. of Agriculture, Washington, 1935), p. 5.

With so many problems involved, neither the solution of any one of them nor general business recovery will alleviate the destitution of any large proportion of the population of the Appalachian-Ozark Area.

LAKE STATES CUT-OVER AREA

Similar in many respects to the Appalachian-Ozark Area is the Lake States Cut-Over Area of northern Michigan, Wisconsin, and Minnesota. Here, too, both mining and lumbering have declined, leaving a stranded population on farms not only small but also largely uncleared. The land is poor at best and the growing season short. Subsistence farming, supplemented by a cash wage, is the most practical type of agriculture for the bulk of the farmers, and the need for rural industries is obvious. In spite of the lack of productivity of the land this is one of the areas in which, as a result of a particularly strong back-to-the-farm movement from urban areas, the number of farms increased most between 1930 and 1935.[12]

The lumber industry has already largely exhausted the virgin timber, leaving only a desert of stumps behind, and it has been found that other regions can produce more economically the basic minerals of this region (iron and copper). Decay of native industries has left an unusually high proportion of nonagricultural workers in need of assistance.

Since the relief problem here is so closely associated with the problem of stranded industrial communities, perhaps no better summing up of the situation in this area could be found than a description of conditions in one of its counties in the fall of 1934 when unemployment was high.

"Almost the entire population of this county is concen-

---

[12] *United States Census of Agriculture: 1935.*

trated around the three mining towns. The only exceptions are one village which owes its existence to logging and sawmill activities and another in which the people are largely dependent on the railroad for their living.

"Only 3 percent of the land in the county is first class land; 52 percent is second class; and 45 percent is third class. Mining and lumbering have been the chief industries in the county with agriculture merely supplementing these two. Some of these so-called farms have practically no land cleared although the same families have lived on them for several years. Those living on the land are first of all miners or woodsmen and are engaging in agriculture solely to supplement their earnings from their usual occupation.

"Even if there should be a large increase in the production of ore, the mines now closed down or working on a part-time basis would not absorb a sufficient number of families to eliminate the relief question. Improved methods of mining have cut the man labor required to approximately one-third of what it used to be, and there would be at least a thousand families who would not be able to regain employment in the mines.

"Logging and the sawmills employ many floaters of the lumberjack type, who come in the winter and go out in the spring. Moreover, the logging industry is gradually petering out.

"All of the unemployed within the county could not find work even if all of the local industries were restored to normal. Only by a very different economic set-up, whose development would take a long period of years, could a solution be found for the 2,000 or more families who appear to be permanently 'thrown over to relief.' " [13]

---

[13] County report, Survey of the Rural Relief Situation, on file in Division of Research, Works Progress Administration.

In such a county the situation of rural youth sixteen through twenty-four years of age is particularly acute. Agriculture offers no opportunities on either the home farm or on neighboring farms, and lumbering is rapidly declining as the cut-over area increases. Such employment as is available in the mines is normally open only to experienced men who have worked there before and been laid off. Whatever the prospects may be for assisting marginal families, the problem of young people in these families should be given special attention.

OTHER RURAL AREAS WITH HIGH RELIEF RATES

Except for the areas laid waste by drought, which are discussed in the next chapter, the major rural problem areas of the nation have been briefly described. Few would deny that they have contained excessive destitution as the result both of long-time factors and of the economic disasters of the last few years. Within each of these areas there are wide gradations of want. Some of their counties may be fairly prosperous while others contain comparatively few rural families with an acceptable standard of living.

This same variation exists, of course, in rural territory elsewhere. In the counties along the South Atlantic and Gulf coasts, in almost all of those in Florida, in numerous scattered counties in the West and Southwest, and in those in the southwestern corner of Pennsylvania rural distress has been intense. While the general factors responsible for rural need have been operative, each smaller area has faced also particular problems caused by its own economy and population characteristics. Before adequate programs for the solution of deep-rooted problems can be developed, the knowledge of the extent and character of these local areas will have to be more accurate than it is at present.

While some localized areas of intense need remain practically as depressed as in the early days of emergency relief, others have improved. Still others, however, are actually in a worse plight than ever before, owing to the effects of the recession of 1937–38 upon an economic set-up which had not recovered from previous disaster.

Although reports from the United States Department of Agriculture record a rise in farm income throughout the past few years, our basic rural problems remain. And they will remain until there is a fundamental and large-scale effort toward solving them—expanding, contracting, and expanding again, as agricultural and general rural-industrial conditions swing from depression to prosperity and back again.

CHAPTER ELEVEN

DROUGHT DISTRESS

THE ENTIRE program for the readjustment of agriculture, after its long depression during the nineteen-twenties and early nineteen-thirties, was sharply interrupted by the series of severe droughts which reached extreme proportions in the summers of 1934 and 1936. In some localities moisture deficiencies have been cumulative since the years of the World War, with short and intermittent rains insufficient to be of lasting benefit. Present drought conditions began early in 1930 and have appeared in one place or another each year since then. Shifting now to the East and now to the West, sometimes to the South and often to the Northwest, the center of dryness has been located most frequently in one section or another of the Great Plains. The areas most often and seriously affected cover large parts of ten of the Great Plains States.

In recent years as one crop failure followed another in parts of the Plains States, the resources of thousands upon thousands of families have dwindled and vanished with the dry, powdered soil blown from their fields. Though in some favored sections there have been fair yields, and though in 1932 and 1935 production approached normal except in scattered dry districts, depression prices for farm products in many instances hardly covered annual charges plus operating expenses. Recurrent drought, insect pests, hail, and plant diseases have harassed the farmer of the plains to the point of desperation.

With personal credit exhausted and the inability of local governments to finance relief programs all too apparent, it became plain early in the present decade that it was a question of federal action or starvation, and during most of the last four years a shockingly large percentage of the approximately fifteen million people who live in and about the vast region called the Great Plains have been obliged to depend almost entirely on public assistance. For the most part, their plight is chargeable primarily to drought. Overwhelmingly an agricultural region, even the larger towns and cities are directly affected by crop and livestock conditions. A destructive drought diminishes the wealth of the entire region, rural and urban.

A REPEATED STORY

The droughts of the nineteen-thirties are not without precedent in any particular except that the extent of suffering has been intensified by recurrent dry years in the same areas. Recent experiences were foretold by the chief hydrographer of the United States some forty years ago, when settlement in most parts of the plains had hardly begun. Mr. Newell wrote:

"Year after year the water supply may be ample, the forage plants cover the ground with a rank growth, the herds multiply, the settlers extend their fields, when, almost imperceptibly, the climate becomes less humid, the rain clouds forming day after day disappear upon the horizon, and weeks lengthen into months without a drop of moisture. The grasses wither, the herds wander wearily over the plains in search of water holes, the crops wilt and languish, yielding not even the seed for another year. Fall and winter come and go with occasional showers which scarcely seem to wet the earth, and the following spring opens with the soil so dry that it is blown about over the windy plains. Another and perhaps another season of drought occurs, the settlers depart with such of their household furniture as can be drawn away by the enfeebled draft animals, the herds disappear, and this beautiful land, once so fruitful, is now dry and brown, given over to the prairie wolf. Then comes a season of ample rains. The prairie grasses, dormant through several seasons, spring into life, and with these the hopes of new pioneers. Then recurs the flood of immigration, to be continued until the next long drought." [1]

From the earliest days of its settlement the West has been menaced by the spectre of drought. Even those sections where the average annual rainfall and its seasonal distribution are most favorable have not escaped an occasional period of protracted dryness, usually accompanied by excessive heat. Two such periods in succession in the same locality were calamitous. But drought was not serious until pioneer agriculture pushed beyond what is considered the realm of safety—the twenty-inch rainfall line, which extends irregularly from the northern junction of North Dakota and Minnesota at the Canadian border, south and slightly west across South Dakota, Nebraska, Kansas, and the Panhandle of Oklahoma to the Rio Grande.

Between this limit of twenty-inch rainfall and the Continental Divide lie the sloping plains containing the Spring Wheat Area, the Winter Wheat Area, part of the Ranching

---

[1] Frederick H. Newell, "Irrigation on the Great Plains," *Yearbook* (U. S. Dept. of Agriculture, 1896), p. 168.

Area, and the dry-land sections of the Western Cotton Area.

These are areas with problems of a different sort from those discussed in the preceding chapter—problems concerned with deficiency of moisture and failure of cultivators to adhere to a system of land use adapted to recurrent drought conditions.

AREAS OF DAMAGE

There are two distinct centers of drought distress in the counties in and around the Great Plains. The northern center begins at the Canadian border and, taking in nearly all of North Dakota and large portions of South Dakota, eastern Montana, northeastern Wyoming, and west central Minnesota, includes the Spring Wheat Area and some ranching and mixed agricultural sections.

It is separated from the southern center by almost the entire state of Nebraska, where drought effects have been of only medium intensity. This southern area is the Dust Bowl proper and includes corners of Kansas, Oklahoma, Colorado, New Mexico, and Texas. It includes the western end of the Winter Wheat Area and extends into a few Corn Belt counties, across the western extremity of the Cotton Belt, and westward into the ranching and mixed agricultural areas of Colorado and New Mexico.

These two regions contain 252 counties, which include nearly one tenth of the nation's land area. Within most of these counties the alleviation of drought distress occasioned from 1933 through 1936 an expenditure of federal funds amounting to $120 or more for each man, woman, and child in the 1930 population. In nearly half of the counties the per capita expenditure was $175 or more.

Usually there is not sufficient diversification to produce

enough of the family living at home to guarantee security. Likewise in time of drought the food crops fail almost as often as cash crops and the stored reserves are negligible. This means that when cash income fails the need for sustenance arises fairly soon. Subsistence for human beings and animals alike then becomes an urgent problem—concerning, first, private organizations, and then, as the drought spreads and its severity increases, local and state governments and philanthropic agencies of national scope, and finally the federal government.

Heretofore, practically all research, both governmental and nongovernmental, into the problems of the Great Plains Region has had a physical approach. Land classification and utilization, soil composition and moisture content, precipitation, wind velocity, erosion, and plant ecology—all have received intensive study, and to a good end.[2] But we are here concerned with the families which have been trying to farm the short grass plains for nearly seventy years. Some have remained, through good years and poor, attempting to acquire through long and painful experience a time-tested technique for the subjugation of nature. Many others have acknowledged failure, salvaged what they could from an unprofitable enterprise, and struck out for other parts to begin anew. Replacements for those who have left will undoubtedly come with the return of favorable crop weather, and the human succession in the dry-land sections of the Great Plains goes on.

STRICKEN PEOPLE

The climatic pulse of the region may be measured, to an extent, by the ebb and flow of its people. The govern-

---

[2] For a comprehensive summary report along these lines, see Report of Great Plains Committee, *The Future of the Great Plains* (Washington, December, 1936). Also see Goodrich, *et al., op. cit.,* Chap. v.

ment's homestead policy and the persuasive speculator drew them into the Plains Area overabundantly, and now each successive drought drives them out by the thousands, disheartened and disillusioned, to settle in other localities. The return of more favorable conditions—a little moisture, some faint promise of a crop—is all that is needed to attract new hopefuls in their places. The recently written history of a western Kansas county [3] shows that periods of extended drought have been associated with important changes in the size and mobility of population. An immediate effect of drought is a cessation of immigration and an acceleration of emigration. But when good crop weather returns, this is reversed and the dirt farmers flow in again. Since 1932 migration away from drought-stricken areas, particularly among the lower economic strata of rural society, has been considerably checked by the extension of federal aid to destitute farm families. To many the meager benefits of the government's rural relief program are preferable to the uncertainty of a new venture in a strange locality. Meanwhile, hope springs eternal of "better luck next year."

The recent droughts and their attendant dust storms have driven much of the population from the Great Plains Area eastward into Minnesota and Iowa and westward into the Pacific States. Many of the hopeless victims have moved on to augment the shifting labor supply of the New Mexico and California orchards and fields. The jobs that formerly fell to Mexican migrants are now largely filled by migrants from Oklahoma and Texas drought areas, anxious for any work no matter how irregular or poorly paid.

Much loose talk has been indulged in about moving all

---

[3] A. D. Edwards, *Influence of Drought and Depression on a Rural Community*, Social Research Report No. VII (U. S. Dept. of Agriculture, Washington, 1938).

the people out of the Dust Bowl of the Southwest. With rational agricultural practices the area is capable of supporting a considerable population. While substitution of field crops for pasture was undoubtedly a mistake in wide areas, still field crops can be grown along the stream beds and grass restored to the higher ridges. A recent study led to the recommendation that 52 per cent of all cultivated and idle land in twenty counties in the heart of the Dust Bowl be returned to a permanent cover of native vegetation. Such a program would not support as large a population as that which was endeavoring to live on the land in 1930 but it would provide economic security for a limited number of families.

Before the general depression of 1932 recurrent drought, with its attendant suffering, was considered a matter of local concern, in the same general category as destitution from other causes. But the unusual combination of industrial depression and agricultural depression and the great severity of the several droughts forced the whole subject sharply into the national consciousness. Since the first grants to states made by the Reconstruction Finance Corporation in 1932, destitution born of drought has been an important part of the relief structure.

RELIEF

From the earliest days of federal assistance the necessity for aid to needy families was intensified in certain areas by drought. The Federal Emergency Relief Administration had been in existence but two weeks when the first petition from drought sufferers was received. So grave a situation existed in the Southwest that, early in June, 1933, the Red Cross, which previously had rendered notable service in this as in other types of disaster, was reluctantly obliged to report that the drought had created emergency needs which exceeded its capacity.

Conditions grew worse in both the northern and southern sections of the Great Plains Region as the summer advanced, and soon government aid was flowing out to areas of distress through many channels. Drought operated to keep relief loads consistently heavy. In February, 1935, the relief load for the Great Plains drought area as a whole included more than one out of every five households. These were headed not only by farmers but also by merchants, doctors, teachers, and many other rural people indirectly dependent upon agriculture. Since crops were fair in 1935, the relief load went down slightly during the winter, but in the winter of 1936, after another severe drought, distress was again acute and considerably more than one out of every five households in this land of dry creek beds and suffocating dust storms was on relief. Furthermore, the families receiving work and direct relief would have been far more numerous if the Agricultural Adjustment Administration, the Resettlement Administration, the Farm Credit Administration, the Federal Surplus Commodities Corporation, and the Soil Conservation Service had not intensified their efforts in the drought areas. A recent survey shows that in sixteen out of twenty-four widely distributed counties in the drought area more than half of all households were recipients of federal aid from one or more of the various relief programs.[4] During the last six months of 1936 more than 85 per cent of all house-

---

[4] Based upon total number of families (which is not always synonymous with households) as reported in the census of 1930. Because of a considerable decrease in the population of many drought counties of the West since the last census, the percentage of households on relief to the total number of families in the last half of 1936 would undoubtedly be much higher.

holds in at least one county in the Northern Great Plains were receiving aid from public funds.

When distress becomes so deep-rooted, one good season will not cure it. Except for certain sore spots, 1937 was a good year agriculturally; yet at its close relief loads in some drought sections were still heavy. In his testimony before the Senate Committee on Unemployment and Relief in January, 1938, Secretary Wallace said:

"In most agricultural regions, 1937 crop production was good and the Farm Security Administration was able to drop from its grant rolls the majority of farmers who had been carried through the winter and spring of 1936–37. However, portions of the States of Montana, Wyoming, North Dakota, South Dakota, Colorado, New Mexico, Kansas, and Nebraska experienced either complete or nearly complete crop failures. Farm families in these areas are in very real need of continued assistance."

Mr. Wallace included with his statement on rural relief needs a list of counties in the states of North Dakota, South Dakota, and Montana in which from 34 to 77 per cent of the farm families were then (January, 1938) receiving emergency subsistence grants from the Farm Security Administration. He also pointed out that the Farm Security Administration lately had been obliged to refuse rehabilitation loans to farmers in localities where the soil did not contain enough moisture to justify planting a crop.

While drought, causing crop failures and loss of livestock, was the major factor in heavy relief loads in the Great Plains, the agricultural depression also did much to swell them as is proved by the length of the relief histories of many applying for assistance. It was found that one out of every eleven agricultural families on relief in the drought area in October, 1935, had received relief during more than twenty-four months since January, 1932. In Montana, one of the states which felt the impact of the 1933 drought, more than two out of five farm relief households had had federal aid for more than two years by October, 1935.[5]

Farm families went on and off relief as their fortunes rose and fell or as the local relief policy permitted. Montana, again, is a good example. In June, 1935, only one sixth of the farmers on relief were receiving aid for the first time and one out of every four farmers had been on relief at least five times.

Although farmers were driven again and yet again to ask for help in their losing battle with the forces of nature, the amount of relief received was woefully inadequate. By the summer of 1935 relief grants were higher in general than in the two preceding years of federal assistance; but, even so, they averaged only seventeen dollars a month per family in the drought area. Yet the fact that aid from other agencies raised the total assistance considerably should be kept in mind.

CHARACTERISTICS OF RELIEF HOUSEHOLDS

The fact that over 90 per cent of the households on relief in the drought area contained persons working or seeking work is evidence that they were victims of circumstances largely beyond their control. Three fourths of those who were usually engaged in agriculture were continuing as farmers and making some attempt to wrest a living from the land.

But these relief farmers were handicapped, even without

---

[5] Irene Link, *Relief and Rehabilitation in the Drought Area*, Special Report, Works Progress Administration, Division of Social Research (Washington, June, 1937), pp. 21, 46.

drought, for many reasons. Their farms were small in an area where large-scale agriculture is the rule. Most of the relief farmers were saddled with rent or taxes and mortgage payments, and they had comparatively large families to feed and clothe. Since many of them were relatively young, their children were too small to be of any assistance financially or even to help with farm work to any great extent.

There is no better indication of the effect of drought than the employment status of farmers. More than one fifth of the agricultural workers in the drought area were unemployed and seeking work in June, 1935—the middle of the crop season in a relatively good year. The situation among farm laborers was even more serious; seven tenths of the total number had lost their jobs. With little or no money with which to hire help for such crops as there were, it is not surprising that farm operators reduced their hired labor to the minimum. Moreover, since nonagricultural prosperity in the western farming area is so largely dependent on agricultural prosperity, there are practically no substitute jobs available to displaced agricultural workers.

The farmers who faced destitution in the drought areas were not newcomers. Most relief clients had settled there long ago. Over half of the farmers in the area had lived in the same county for twenty years or more. Only one in eight had moved into the drought area since 1930.

Case history after case history could be cited to illustrate the plight of farmers who have spent the best years of their lives within the area. The Stevens household is typical— father, mother, and three children. After fifteen years of farming in their present county and the one adjoining, Stevens purchased, in 1930, a dry-land farm of 160 acres.

Equipped with adequate buildings, it was valued at that time at $1,500. In 1935 when the family first applied for relief, the Federal Land Bank still held a $1,200 mortgage in spite of depreciated values. Other debts, including delinquent taxes, came to an additional $250. The family had managed to remain self-sustaining through the droughts of 1933 and 1934 but repeated crop failures and lack of opportunities for employment finally proved too much for their slender resources. At the time of application for relief in the summer of 1935, the family's only cash income was a weekly cream check of approximately $1.25. But assisted through the winter of 1935–36, they were again able to become self-sufficient with the beginning of a new farming season. However, their independence was short-lived, for crops failed again in 1936, once more forcing them to seek federal aid. By this time their situation was even less secure by reason of an additional burden of debts amounting to more than $500. Yet the Stevens family is industrious. All that is needed to put them back on their feet is a year or two of good crops and opportunities for supplementary cash income from work off the farm.

There have been many photographs of the devastation wrought by drought and dust storms. Some of them have shown families like the Stevens; and some have been taken of people in even more desperate straits. The condition of farmers in a county in North Dakota is described here as an illustration of what can happen to an entire county when it suffers from successive dry years.

In May, 1935, almost 89 per cent of the farmers in the county were on relief, and more than half of them had been on relief since 1933. The distress of farmers in this area was intensified by the fact that they were largely dependent for their cash income on crop sales which in 1934 brought them nothing. In that year farmers' gross cash incomes averaged only $623 per farm, and about three fourths of this came from the government—livestock sales in the cattle purchase program, payments on crop production control contracts, and emergency relief grants. Only about one fifth of this cash income came from the sale of livestock (exclusive of livestock sold to the government) and from livestock products. Miscellaneous sources accounted for the remaining 6 per cent.

By May, 1935, outstanding feed and seed loan indebtedness in the county averaged $866 per farm. Almost 50 per cent of the farm land was mortgaged for an average of $13 per acre, or 87 per cent of the census evaluation of land and buildings. A large proportion of all of the taxes that had been delinquent from 1927 to 1933 remained unpaid on four fifths of the total acreage. Tenancy had increased greatly in the county. In 1920 only one seventh of the farmers were tenants, but by 1935 more than one third of the operators were paying rent for their farms—many of them for farms that they had owned a few years back.[6]

The summary which revealed these conditions was made in the summer of 1935 when the agricultural situation had improved somewhat. Then, 1936 brought another major drought, adding fresh disaster to this already prostrate county.

The drought had equally as disastrous effects on other regions of the Great Plains. Rural distress was acute in the entire North Plains of Texas in 1935 as a result of a prolonged period of deficient rainfall. Fields in certain sandy loam localities were so damaged by wind erosion as to be of questionable future value. A number of farmers

---

[6] Kifer and Stewart, *op. cit.*, Chap. 1.

had abandoned their farms, and many who remained were in a miserable plight. Mortgages had become so heavy that in many instances farmers were carrying a debt approximately equal to, and sometimes greater than, the current value of their farms.

Even when rains or snows occur in areas previously visited by severe drought, the need for assistance does not cease. After a land has been seared by successive droughts, the ground is so dry that water runs off instead of sinking in, and it takes several seasons of normal or above-normal rainfall to restore the soil moisture to required levels. In many cases much of the topsoil has blown away in the recent dry years, leaving unbroken subsoil strongly resistant to water. Moreover, reservoirs and stream beds have often dried up completely and their volume and flow are not quickly restored to normal. In many instances the water table has sunk below previously recorded levels.

Naturally, with the slow restoration of normal moisture content, the productivity of the land is affected. After a serious drought, crops cannot attain former production figures in one season. In the case of natural pastures, after a dry period, several years of average rainfall are often necessary before they can support as many head of livestock as before.

Farmers and those engaged in supplying the wants of farmers have been aided by government subsidies, either directly or indirectly, since early in 1932. Assistance in some form must continue. As to how long, opinions differ. To the extent that a public works program is relied on, account must be taken of the fact that during much of the year the farmer must be free to tend his fields. Otherwise his rehabilitation on the land will not succeed.

CHAPTER TWELVE

RELIEF AND RECONSTRUCTION

ALLEVIATION OF open country and village distress cost private welfare agencies and federal and local governments over three and one-half billion dollars in the seven years 1931 through 1937. Much of the distress which these expenditures helped alleviate has been shown to be preventable, and all possible measures should be taken to guarantee that the situation which caused that distress shall not arise again. Even disregarding the human privation and suffering involved it would be cheaper from an economic standpoint to spend modest sums on prevention in good times than to be compelled to make such vast outlays after acute distress has developed. It is also healthier for the industry and the trade of the nation to keep workers engaged in productive enterprise and to maintain purchasing power, for when incomes of the rural people shrink the purchasing power of the nation is greatly impaired.

In terms of prices the agricultural depression began in 1921; some of the more subtle difficulties of rural credit began earlier; and forest and soil assets have been frittered away by our national policies over a long period. For these reasons the agricultural depression antedated the industrial depression by a decade. Since the resulting human distress is longstanding, it is evident that the passing of a financial crisis will not restore rural life to the vigorous position which it occupied in the previous century. More than emergency action is needed. A long-range plan of attack not subject to emergency psychology should be the goal.

CHANGES IN PUBLIC OPINION

The depression and the resultant recovery programs did inject new elements into the situation. The positive efforts of the federal government to meet the emergency undermined the previous policy of leaving the fate of rural people to individual and local initiative. It has been clearly established that the well-being of such a large segment of the working population is of sufficient concern to warrant concerted, constructive action. Not only are the farmers and villagers an important element of the nation's producers, but they and their families also constitute nearly half of the nation's consumers. The discussions growing out of the crisis have re-emphasized the mutual dependence of the farm family and the industrial family.

The depression and the extension of relief to rural areas has uncovered and revealed to the country the extent of rural distress. That there were destitute people on the land had been only dimly realized before, and there was practically no realization of the problems of rural industrial workers. As soon as the means of extending relief in the country became systematic, it appeared that almost as high a proportion of the people were in need in problem counties as in cities and that in many counties the distress was even more shocking. The nation is becoming increasingly aware that rural slums are as disturbing in their squalor as their counterparts in cities.

CHANGES IN AGRICULTURE

American agriculture has exhibited two stages, the pioneering and the exploitative, and neither stage is now contributing to the national welfare. In the pioneering stage the "younger sons" who were not needed at home or who did not go into industry marched across the continent, putting their energies into the acquisition of land. The history of a typical family shows that it originated in Massachusetts, and that one branch subsequently moved across Ohio in two stages; thence some went to Montana and others to Nebraska; and now one offshoot is in California. At each stage the pioneer member wrested his farm from nature and was content that part of the profits of his enterprise should accrue from the rise in land values which came about as civilization overtook his outpost. For a long period of time the surplus earnings of the farmers on the frontier fringe went into land. They were literally plowing back their profits into increased land values.

Behind the pioneers came the exploiters in those sections where cash crops proved profitable. The quick profits to be made from tobacco and cotton in the South and corn and wheat in the Midwest hypnotized the holders of land into a belief in the system of mining out the fertility of their fields. This has left only a few sections of the country with a balanced agriculture and a rural life built for stability. The process has been wasteful of forest and water resources alike and damaging to the land. It has gradually concentrated masses of disadvantaged men in definite areas —disadvantaged in making a living, in transportation, in land tenure, and in public health and educational facilities. A new orientation is imperative if there is to be a healthy balance between city and country and a vigorous rural life.

Those who think exclusively of the physical or the economic aspects of agriculture are often prone to dismiss these disadvantaged classes with the statement that they are weaklings—a permanently submerged class which will continue to be a burden to relief agencies. The humanitarian does not adopt such a defeatist attitude nor does he shrug this problem aside so arbitrarily. Trained in observation of human traits and institutions he realizes that many of these people suffer from social, personal, and economic defects that can be remedied. The foregoing pages have established the relationship of dependency to educational disadvantage, to health hazards, to family disorganization, and to disadvantages in land tenure. Certainly these are human handicaps subject to removal by an enlightened system of social institutions and a determination to promote a balanced society.

RELIEF AND EMERGENCY EMPLOYMENT

Progress toward the attainment of such human goals has proceeded slowly. The first immediate necessity was to prevent actual want, and this was done by a program of direct relief. From the beginning of the Federal Emergency Relief Administration in 1933 the increase in rural cases was rapid. In 1934 there were over a million and a half rural relief families and at the peak early in 1935 there were approximately two and a half million.

The very variety of programs which have been attempted indicates how complicated and technical is the task of public assistance. The Federal Emergency Relief Administration, the Civil Works Administration, and the Works Progress Administration dealt with the problems of direct and work relief. The programs of the Civilian Conservation Corps and the National Youth Administration were aimed at the needs of young people. Aid to the aged, to the blind, and to dependent children was instituted for those special categories through the Social Security Board; and the Rehabilitation, Subsistence Homesteads, Resettlement, and Farm Security programs were designed to meet the needs of farmers. The history and programs of these varied organizations make a fascinating study, but one too long for inclusion here. This summary will treat only the general aspects of these attempts to reduce the burden of relief.

The final forms of long range relief policies have not been determined. Only Congress can determine them, and it is just beginning to grapple with the fundamentals. Relief has been handled as an emergency activity on a temporary basis. Each fiscal year Congress and the administration have bickered in a semiamicable fashion about the amount to be appropriated. There has been comparatively little informed public discussion and understanding of the issues involved.

Consequently, relief agencies have operated on a hand-to-mouth basis with little continuity of program. The policy makers of the nation are faced with the inescapable fact that unemployment on a fairly large scale is not to be banished quickly and that a long-time constructive program is the only efficient way to cope with it.

To absorb the unemployed workers accumulating during several years of depression, it will be necessary for industry to go beyond its previous high peak, so that it may not only re-employ its former workers but also employ those who have recently matured to working age. This phenomenon of a faster increase in the working population than in the total population will continue for several decades and the end of each slump in employment will find the labor market faced not only with the previously unemployed but also with the new crop of young people. Even when business and industry are booming, there are dislocations caused by migrating industries, and the substitution of machines for men causes unemployment. It is frequently argued that mechanization creates more jobs than it destroys. This, for the sake of argument, may be granted; yet it may readily be established that the advent of the machine brings a serious, even if more or less temporary, maladjustment in the lives of many individuals. Since the jobs created by the machine are not in the same occupation and seldom in the same locality as the jobs destroyed, there follows the necessity of migration and retraining, and often the demotion of the old workers. This is especially true of mechanization in agriculture which is likely to increase the demand for workers in the city and to decrease the demand for farm workers.

The general public has not yet realized that a certain amount of unemployment is a normal phenomenon of the present economic system instead of the result of a passing emergency. Potential workers usually exceed the effective demand, and it is only when the unemployed group becomes excessive that it creates a real problem. Also, the tendency has been to consider anyone not working in industry, trade, or agriculture as not employed productively. There has, however, always been a large group of professional and public servants not engaged in agriculture or industry. The army of post-office employees, nurses, teachers, doctors, and lawyers compose a group rendering necessary services. If the efficiency of the process of producing goods continues to increase, it is inevitable that the numbers available for professional, personal, and public service will increase, and the surplus wealth produced which can be devoted to public welfare will likewise increase.

Out of the past experience one of the basic principles to appear has been that relief of unemployables and of employables, even though these groups shade into one another, are separate, specialized processes. Their differentiation has begun. Unemployables falling into such special categories as the aged, the blind, and dependent children have become the wards of the Social Security Program, and people temporarily or permanently unemployable on account of ill-health, mental incapacity, or other misfortune have again become the wards of local and state relief organizations. To these should probably be added all youth up to eighteen years of age, who should be kept out of the labor market by encouragement to remain in school if at all possible or otherwise to work on public projects, such as the Civilian Conservation Corps and the National Youth Administration work projects, which act as training centers.

Under the Federal Emergency Relief Administration program direct relief grants to the individual household were made on the basis of budgetary deficiency, and the basic budget varied considerably from one section to another, depending on the standard and cost of living. The proportion of the minimum budgetary requirement which was met from relief grants varied with the size of the family and the proportion of its needs which could be procured from supplementary sources, such as farm and garden or part-time job.

It is natural to expect that people with access to the land would need smaller amounts of assistance than urban families, since they have in the land a basis of stability. Also, the frequent ownership of, or nominal rental charge for, many rural houses and the availability of farm produce reduce the need for relief. As a result rural grants averaged considerably less than urban grants, and open country grants were less than those in villages. Also, the type of relief given helped to determine the size of the grant. Thus, in February, 1935, the range of variation was from less than four dollars for Negro croppers on direct relief in the South to about twenty-seven dollars for farm owners on work relief in the Lake States Cut-Over Area.

Grants were considerably higher in most states in 1935 than they were at the beginning of the program in 1933. The adequacy of relief grants was in large measure determined by administrative policies in the various states and by the amount of funds available. One effect of the operations of the Federal Emergency Relief Administration was the application of constant pressure on low standard states to increase their minimum grants, and as a result there was a gradual rise in the amount given to each family during the operation of the federal relief program.

The return of general and direct relief to state support has meant a marked decline in adequacy of grants in some of the poorer states. In December, 1937, eight rural states were making average general relief grants of less than ten dollars per month per family. Nor does this tell the full story, since funds were so limited in some states that a large proportion of their destitute were not granted any relief whatsoever.

Security wages under the Works Program were higher than relief grants. For unskilled workers they ranged from $21 to $60 per month, depending on the section of the country. Wages in rural counties were established uniformly below urban rates. The average wage payment on the Works Program has been $50 to $55 per month or, if the worker has remained on the program for a full year, about $600.

Since 1935 all employables have been considered eligible for work relief under the Works Program, and in addition those farmers with prospects for success have been eligible for rehabilitation loans under the Resettlement and Farm Security administrations. It has not been possible, however, to relocate all relief farmers on the land on account of shortage of loan funds, shortage of administrative personnel necessary for the relocation process, and in some areas lack of prospects for a successful crop. In certain areas large numbers of people with farm backgrounds have remained on direct relief or work programs. In November, 1937, although several hundred thousand farmers had been removed from the relief rolls, thousands of others were receiving Farm Security emergency grants or wages under the Works Program. The distribution of the rural public assistance load at that time, excluding Farm Security loan cases, was: WPA, 40 per cent; Farm Security grants, 6 per cent; aid to the aged, to the blind, and to dependent children, 39 per cent; and state and local general relief, 15 per cent.[1] In some sections a large proportion of WPA workers had farm backgrounds.

The chief argument against work relief and in favor of direct relief boils down to the greater expense of paying workers a security wage as against a smaller direct relief subsistence grant and the additional expense of supervision and materials incident to a work program.

---

[1] Statement of Corrington Gill in *Hearings Before a Special Committee to Investigate Unemployment and Relief, United States Senate,* 75th Cong., 1st sess., II, 1000.

Over against this, the proponents of work relief urge that the program produces improvements of a permanent nature, such as playgrounds, streets, roads, airports, public buildings, and soil and water conserving projects, the cost of which is not properly chargeable as expense since a substantial portion of these improvements is in the nature of additions to the nation's capital. Also, the proponents of work relief contend that the more substantial payments to workers form a greater bulwark of purchasing power and thus stimulate business and industry and maintain the morale of the relief families.

The degree to which the federal budget can stand the large outlays for work relief depends to some extent on the controversial question as to what proportion of the costs of community improvements should be financed from local funds and what proportion from federal funds. Any flat formula for this division of financial responsibility is difficult to apply equitably since the communities where the need is greatest are likely to be those whose public finances can least stand additional appropriations for public improvements.

One difficulty in the way of securing substantial local contributions to work projects during the depression of the early thirties was the fact that a vast number of counties and municipalities had overextended themselves for public works during boom times and had come into the depression with exhausted credit. Others, the ones needing public improvements most, did not have the tax resources to finance them even in good times. Further thinking needs to be done in this field with respect to the establishment of a permanent program of public works and services to meet the variations in the burden of unemployment, the determination of the types of projects to be undertaken, and the extent to which local communities should share in the costs thereof.

The same arguments for work relief that apply to the city apply to the village and other rural-nonfarm segments of the population. From the narrower viewpoint of the farm, however, certain elasticity must be provided. The goal of any constructive program for the relief of farmers should be to establish or reinstate them in productive agriculture. This can be best accomplished under certain conditions by rehabilitation loans and under others by work relief. In sparsely settled counties or in those with scattered relief families it is often extremely difficult to operate work projects efficiently. Normally, for the farmer who has prospects of becoming self-sustaining, the best place is on the land, where he can preserve his agricultural skill and his assets. He can best be kept on the land by a loan either for production purposes or for living expenses. On the other hand, in a period of flood or extreme drought it may not be practical to extend loans for making crops but may be desirable to maintain the farmer on the land by means of work relief or direct grants. Thus, relief for farmers should be projected with a considerable degree of elasticity, the backbone of the scheme being a rehabilitation plan to restore as large a number as possible to self-support while making allowance for work projects designed to fit the agricultural situation, the numbers on relief, and the needs of the community.

REHABILITATION

To support a half-million farmers and a quarter of a million farm laborers by charity neither adds to their agricultural skill nor preserves their agricultural assets. It was, therefore, natural that specialization in relief measures for farmers should begin early and that, where possible, rehabilitation loans should be granted instead of direct relief. The principal difference between this new type of credit—the rehabilitation loan—and former types is that, while under the old types credit was extended on the basis of bankers' security, rehabilitation credit is extended on the basis of the needs of the family and its prospects for rehabilitation on the farm.

The three factors which have enabled the rehabilitation program to extend this type of loan with a gratifying percentage of repayments have been the spreading of the risk over hundreds of thousands of borrowers, careful selection of such borrowers as would make good risks, and, more important, adequate supervision of the operations of borrowers. The loan was accompanied by a service of a type not available from commercial agencies. Farm supervisors advised about methods of using the land and of crop rotation and home supervisors helped with family problems and gave instruction in the canning and preservation of foods. This is in effect a gigantic and well-planned system of adult education in that it teaches the essentials of better living to those who need it most.

The belief which is sometimes expressed that rural relief people constitute a permanently submerged group is not borne out by the results of the rehabilitation program. Although two years is a comparatively short time in which to rehabilitate those who were as unfortunate as the clients who were chosen from the relief rolls, the Farm Security Administration in 1937 reported that about 10 per cent had paid their loans in full before maturity and that collections amounted to a substantial proportion of amounts due. Since most of the loans are recoverable, this is evidently a form of relief which is most economical to the government.

A recent survey of 230,000 such rehabilitation borrowers showed that from the granting of the loan through the 1937 crop year they had increased their average net worth by $253, or a grand total of $58,000,000.[2] But the rehabilitation of these families cannot be measured in terms of money alone. One who has visited them and seen their pride in their homes, their animals, and their stored and canned food keenly feels the strengthened morale and determination of these formerly down-and-out farm families.

PREVENTION OF DISTRESS

Basic to any program of social reconstruction in rural life is the search for a stable agriculture, a national production which will be geared to the markets for agricultural commodities and to the conservation of the great land assets of the nation, and which will enrich the human aspects of rural life. The groundwork of progress in this direction has been laid. In the past few years programs— often admittedly experimental—have ranged all the way from purchase and retirement of submarginal lands from agriculture through programs of soil conservation to efforts to adapt production to market realities by crop control, and thereby to achieve price parity for the farmer.

Regional Aspects.—It is apparent in a country so vast and varied as the United States that the task of agricultural reconstruction has to be undertaken regionally with an eye to fusing varied regional economics into a national whole. This is not simple, since the interests of the various regions do not always conform. Midwest dairy farmers look with apprehension upon any substantial increase in livestock as a means of balancing the cotton economy. Again, the

---

[2] Statement by Secretary of Agriculture Henry A. Wallace in *ibid.*, p. 1126.

subsistence farmers of New England who did not benefit markedly from agricultural adjustment payments complain that their meat, flour, and clothing costs were increased by the operation of the program in other regions. The Program Planning Division of the Agricultural Adjustment Administration and the state agricultural colleges are concerned with this difficult and complex task and may be expected eventually to work out a national regionally balanced agriculture. It is not, however, something to be accomplished in a day.

Crop Control.—The point where the economic reconstruction of agriculture bears most directly upon the reclamation of human beings is in the policy of acreage or crop control. In many areas wheat, cotton, tobacco, and livestock are produced by large-scale operations. Secretary Wallace, in speaking of the California fruit and vegetable districts of the Pacific Coast, the wheat fields of the Great Plains, the Corn Belt, and large areas of the cotton country, stated: "Farming in these parts of the United States is ceasing to be a way of life and is becoming a new kind of highly organized industry. The dominant type of farm in some of these areas no longer is a family-sized homestead; it is a great outdoor factory, built around labor-saving machinery which can be operated by gangs of seasonal workers." [3] Therefore, reduction in volume of production means reduction in man-power needs. Such farms, like factories, lay off help when production is curtailed. This is not the situation in balanced general farming areas where commercial production is more widely scattered among a large number of small producers. In such areas a decrease

---

[3] Excerpt from a statement by Secretary of Agriculture Wallace in *Hearings Before a Special Committee to Investigate Unemployment and Relief, United States Senate,* I, 335.

in commercial production, accompanied by a slight increase in home-consumed food or feed, makes the farmer's income larger and relatively more stable. One of the most significant findings in a recent study of cotton tenancy was that, whereas the landlord's income increased in proportion to the amount of cotton planted, the tenant's income increased in proportion to his production of foodstuffs for home use. Thousands of small commercial farmers could obtain a material improvement in level of living if they inclined more toward live-at-home farming. Moreover, experience has shown that it is the small farmer, operating his own acres, who conserves the soil most effectively.

One way out is, in general, to apply production restrictions slightly more strongly on the larger producers than on the smaller ones, leaving leeway for new entrants to secure small quotas of commercial crops and to concentrate largely on live-at-home and general farming. This would reduce the concentration of commercialized farm areas and increase the areas of balanced general farming.

The makers of agricultural policy need to consider carefully possibilities for more intensive use of the land in those sections where balanced general farming is favored by soil and climate and where some of the increase in agricultural population could be located on good land. A primary objective of rural policies should be adaptation of its population to the land resources of the nation. Population trends up to 1980 have been predicted within reasonable limits of accuracy on the assumption of high, medium, or low fertility rates. These predictions tell us within limits what the labor supply will be and what the probable demand for food should be if we assume that every person is assured an adequate diet.

Poverty and Plenty.—At present large groups are grievously undernourished, although this is in a land whose productive capacity is seemingly limitless. Such conditions in the midst of potential plenty are a blot upon democratic institutions. A partial answer to this enigma is the reorganization of the system of distribution whereby the poor and undernourished may secure the essentials of a balanced diet at a lower cost. Sweden has experimented with this on the assumption that it is better to give her own poor the benefit of subsidies than to give these benefits to foreign purchasers by dumping surpluses at a low price. The United States has tried free distribution through the Federal Surplus Commodities Corporation, but the relatively small scale of its operations has had comparatively little effect either on surpluses or on dietary deficiencies. In spite of the practical difficulties of administering such a system, a democracy should be depended on to nourish its citizens, especially when the poorer classes are rearing the future population.

Co-operative Farms.—In order to secure the benefits of mechanization and the economies of large-scale management practices and at the same time to preserve an equitable distribution of farm income, it has been proposed that co-operatively owned and managed farms be established. Private enterprise has established one large co-operative farm in the Mississippi Delta, and several of the resettlement projects of the Farm Security Administration are experimenting with co-operative features. It is, however, too early to make an appraisal of the success of these efforts.

There can be little doubt of the similarity of the economic arrangements of the plantation share tenant and those of the worker on a co-operative farm. The share tenant has his crop planned, his feed, seed, and supplies furnished, and works under supervision and for a share of the crop.

The fundamental differences between his status and that of a member of a co-operative farm community is that the tenant does not have any voice in management policies and receives a smaller proportion of the total income.

Farm Prices.—Among the most effective economic measures have been those to secure higher prices for farmers. Whether the rank and file of farmers will continue to constitute a substantially prosperous segment of the population will be determined largely by the success or failure of efforts to adjust their share of the national income.

Few students of farm prices will deny the need for measures to control ungovernable surpluses of farm commodities. Farmers themselves have tried to do this in a rough way by voluntary methods. It has been true for a number of years that farmers after a period of low prices usually adjust their acreage downward and after a period of high prices increase it. Unfortunately, as this adjustment must be made by the unco-ordinated efforts of hundreds of thousands of producers scattered over vast areas, the net result has not always been rational and has tended to exaggerate either underproduction or overproduction as the pendulum approached the end of a swing.

A year or two of overproduction and resultant low prices often displace more labor in commercial farming than does artificial restriction of production. This tendency was manifest in 1921, 1930, 1931, and the winter of 1937–38. In these periods farmers who operated on credit found their funds exhausted at a time when bank credit was restricted, and they were compelled to curtail operations and reduce the number of their laborers or tenants.

This, then, is the dilemma. American agriculture, to maintain balance in the national picture and to accommodate part of the increase in rural population, must eventually be geared to expansion. Yet surpluses of commercial crops and restriction of foreign markets point to the necessity for control of commercial crop output for at least a period of years.

A full recovery of industry with some additional foreign trade would contribute materially to the removal of agricultural surplus. With a considerably increased national income and a greater share of the purchasing power in the hands of low income families the nation need not concern itself with overproduction since billions of dollars worth of foods and fibres are needed to bring the level of living of low income families up to a minimum standard. This is a goal worth striving for and one by no means beyond the energy and inventiveness of the American people.

The unknown factors in future agricultural expansion are the possible introduction of new farm products, the expanding use of agricultural products in industry, the development of new industries, the fluctuations in foreign trade, and the extent to which the use of machines and other technical improvements will increase the productivity per man and hence restrict the numbers required to produce the necessary foods and fibres. From the known elements a policy of population guidance should be evolved which would acquaint the inexperienced youth and unemployed worker with the needs for varied occupations and with areas of expanding opportunity and which would warn them of blind-alley jobs and depressed localities.

Population Policy.—Of especial urgency is a rational population policy in the drought areas and the cotton South. These are both areas of rapid population increase and limited opportunity under the present system of agriculture. Barring radical shifts in the agricultural system, heavy migration from the farms in these areas must continue. Enough children are already born to cause heavy pressure on opportunity in these sections for the next twenty years.

The greatest migration of modern times occurred between 1920 and 1930 when thousands from all over the nation were lured to California by the chambers of commerce, the real-estate boosters, and their own visualizations of a superior place in which to work and live. But it was sadly overdone. In many cases the result was bitter disappointment. Noting the load of relief arising from the thousands of disillusioned settlers, the Californians, during the depression, have endeavored to turn people back at the border and have used every device to reverse the flow. There could be no clearer instance of the folly of individual, unguided movement. More thorough study of the occupational outlook in various areas is necessary, and the dissemination of information thus obtained in areas of excess population is a basic need for the rational distribution of population.

Land-Use Planning.—Another important connection between the physical and the human elements in agricultural reconstruction is in the field of land-use planning. The use of land in the past has been too largely determined by the speculator who has been active from colonial days to the present time, ever ready to buy cheap and sell dear after he has raised false hopes. Land planning on its largest scale involves the determination of optimum uses for land in the major regions of the country. Especially difficult problems are presented in this respect in the cotton and drought areas. Overuse of the land for commercial crops has brought both areas to a low level of agricultural production which needs thorough reorganization.

On a smaller scale land-use planning involves the re-

FSA, USDA

Rehabilitated

WPA

The Millionth WPA Pupil

tirement from agriculture of lands which have deteriorated so far as to be below the level of profitable use and adaptation of these lands to grazing, forests, or public park and recreation purposes. Some beginning has been made in this respect in the purchase of lands by the Resettlement Administration.

Erosion.—Cultivation which removed all ground cover for most of the year has caused millions of acres of farm land to erode to the danger point, and efforts to make a living from such land are now precarious and will become more and more so if present practices are continued. The most fundamental approach to the conservation of agricultural resources is the program of the Soil Conservation Service for combatting such erosion. Its efforts are directed both toward re-creation of the fertility of already seriously eroded lands and the preservation of the fertility of lands endangered through overcropping.

Russell Lord recently prefaced an article on erosion by the following: "Do you know that our terrible floods and our terrible dust storms have exactly the same cause? That they are both our own fault? That they will quickly ruin America if we don't stop them? And that we can conquer them only if we act *now?*"[3a]

Rural Industries.—The widespread effects of the breakdown of rural industries have been discussed in the chapter on relief in village areas. Rural destitution was particularly acute in areas of decadent lumbering and mining operations. The possibilities for the resumption of such operations in these communities are slight. Most of them will continue as "ghost towns" until the last resident departs or dies. All trends point to an increase in the number of

---

[3a] "Watching the Farms Go By," in *Hearst's International-Cosmopolitan,* CIV (June, 1938), 36.

such towns as raw materials are further exhausted. Technological changes will continue to displace workers and their reabsorption into other lines of work may be expected to be slow since neither lumbering nor mining experience makes them readily adaptable to other pursuits. An increasing premium will probably be placed on younger workers. The problems created relate not only to full-time miners and lumbermen but also to the numerous farmers who in the past have relied upon part-time work in the mines and mills to provide a cash income with which to supplement returns from the farm.

There is also the problem of the small manufacturing plant in rural areas. During the depression one such establishment after another was closed down. The importance of such enterprises to rural well-being is becoming increasingly apparent. Experience has shown that the movement of industry to rural areas is uncertain and that plans posited on the development of such industry may easily be over-optimistic. Nor can its stability be guaranteed after it has moved in. A definite trend toward the migration of industry to the rural South, however, has been in process. Where a number of favorable factors are found in a rural area, industries may be expected to move in.

The promotion of a combination of farming and rural industrial enterprise was extensively suggested at the beginning of the depression as a method of cushioning the effect of underemployment or unemployment. Some increase in this combined activity actually took place. It is evident, however, that commercial farmers gain little from attempting to earn wages in industry although members of their families may profitably do so. Industrial workers who have the spare time or unemployed members of their families can manifestly profit from the cultivation of gardens or the raising of domestic animals if they live on the land. The expansion of this type of combined activity is contingent, however, upon the further decentralization of industry and its location where land is available. Such spread of industry has progressed rather slowly except around the rim of large industrial areas, and the prospects of rapid expansion are not bright for the immediate future.

Tenancy.—Any program of adapting population to the land should especially consider the problem of tenancy, which increases in importance as the pressure of population on land becomes more severe and as farms become more difficult to own. A certain amount of tenancy, especially among young farmers just starting out, is inevitable and desirable, but when tenancy increases rapidly at the expense of ownership and when a class develops whose members remain tenants throughout their lifetime, whose daughters marry tenants, and whose sons also become lifelong tenants, the situation grows socially vicious, especially when tenancy assumes such dependency as is involved in the share-cropper arrangement.

The recommendations of the recent Committee on Farm Tenancy suggested two courses: first, the improvement of the condition of those who are tenants and, second, assistance to tenants who are ambitious and able to become landowners.

The measures for improving the condition of tenants aside from those designed to increase their productivity center largely on the improvement of lease forms—the insistence on written contracts, the formulation of sharing arrangements based on diversified crop production, and the protection of both the tenant and the landlord in respect to their interest in improvements made in the land and buildings. In this respect England is a century ahead of us, since she has not only protected the landlord-tenant relationship thoroughly by laws governing the lease but has also developed a system of special land courts for dealing with cases arising under these laws.

With this protection the majority of English farmers prefer to remain tenants, using their capital for production goods and wages. Land under this system has become a fairly stable low income returning investment, yielding around 4 to 5 per cent and offering little speculative inducement. Thus, in some respects, what this country needs is not so much a smaller proportion of tenants as a different type of tenure.

For inexperienced youth and tenants who would become owners, a period of testing is essential for the selection of those whose ambition and ability to become capable managers of farm enterprises are sufficient for success. It is not enough to place a man who wants to farm on a good piece of land. He must have certain farming experience and skills or must have careful supervision until he acquires them. He must be able to plan for the most efficient use of his land, for the conservation and restoration of fertility, for the accumulation of livestock and equipment. He must know where and when to dispose of his produce. It takes resourcefulness, initiative, and managerial ability to farm successfully—qualities in little demand by the urban worker who performs a routine job. Farming is not simply a way of life; it is a business entered into by a family, and misfits are many and serious. The sooner it is realized that not everyone can farm and that many of those who can farm, particularly those whose experience has been wholly as share croppers, should never be owners but should always till the land under supervision, the nearer we shall come to a sound system of agricultural employment. The rehabilitation program of loans and supervisory service should provide a testing ground for landless men who have the requisites for efficient farming.

For those who show promise of success during such a period of testing, the Farm Security Administration is making a modest beginning in assistance toward the purchase of farms. The small appropriation under which this program operates will provide for valuable experimentation in this field, but it is not sufficient to assist any large proportion of tenants in attaining ownership except over a long period of time. In fact the number who can be supplied with units averaging four thousand dollars in value under this appropriation is hardly equal to the annual increase in tenants under present conditions.

Housing.—An effective rural housing program is another method of improving the level of living of thousands of farm families. It would also contribute materially to the absorption of the rural unemployed. The practical difficulties in the way of such a program, however, are far greater than in the case of urban housing. Houses for rent in rural areas are not concentrated in large numbers as in the city, and the financing of scattered construction is extremely difficult. Furthermore, the inducement of private owners to build with liberal government credit is limited by the productivity of the land. Many farms, as at present operated, do not produce enough to provide large sums for capital improvement.

Education.—Since the population increase of the nation is coming largely from farms and villages, especially from the farms and villages of the poorest sections, the problems of children and youth in those areas are deserving of particular attention. The national welfare demands that these future citizens be given as good educational facilities as is consistent with the national economy. National public interest obviously demands the equalization through federal funds of educational opportunities for the future workers of America regardless of the financial condition of the area in which they are reared. There is no more potent method of raising the rural level of living than education. The evils of an excessive birth rate, malnutrition and disease, and unsanitary living conditions are some of the most obvious ones which would be ameliorated.

The gap between the time of leaving school and the time of settling into a more or less permanent occupation is a particularly critical period for youth, especially for those rural youth who spend a year or two as unpaid helpers on the family farm. Whether to remain in agriculture or to seek a vocation in industry or trade is a vital question— settled all too often by chance. This after-school period is one in which the agencies of adult education and vocational guidance have an especially important function to perform, a function which is now almost wholly inoperative in rural communities. Employment studies emphasize the difficulty of placing untrained workers, those with neither skill nor experience to offer, in the labor market.

Not only is there need for stronger school facilities but also the broader task of adult education needs to be more effectively undertaken in rural areas. It should be evident that in a democracy legislative schemes merely create a situation within which the individual has the opportunity to better himself. The extent to which the individual actually benefits by this opportunity will depend on his energy and intelligence. Lack of basic knowledge is the primary handicap of many farmers today both in their farming and in their community relationships. They stand in great need of the kind of advice and instruction given

by farm and home demonstration agents. These and all
other methods of instruction in the betterment of farm,
home, and community need to be made widely available in
rural districts. Without a citizenry intelligent with respect
to these matters no amount of remedial legislation will cure
the ills of democracy.

Health.—Aside from education and related facilities,
there is a noticeable deficiency in rural public health programs. The natural health and vitality of rural people are
equal to or greater than those of urban dwellers, but that
does not mean that there is not a great deal of preventable
sickness and loss of employment due to ill-health. At
present somewhat less than one third of the rural population of the average state is served by full-time health units
and in over three fourths of the states less than 50 per cent
is so served. It has been estimated that fewer than fifty
counties have health services comparable to those in most
up-to-date municipalities.

Sufficient experience has been accumulated to show that
adequate health services for rural areas are possible at relatively low cost. Small hospitals to meet the demands of
local communities are needed particularly. Traveling
clinics for the examination and treatment of school children, and even adults, have long since proved their worth.
In spite of the naturally more healthful living conditions
of the country the rank and file of the people, with little
or no money to spend on remedial treatment, are in some
ways worse off than urban dwellers who long have had
available the services provided by excellent clinics.

Financing Rural Services.—The financing in rural areas
of relief, educational, and public health services, so essential in the promotion of the general welfare, is largely
dependent on the equalization of the distribution of tax

money within states between cities and rural districts and within the nation between states of great wealth and states of little wealth. States without large financial or industrial centers actually do not control within their boundaries the wealth requisite for adequate support of up-to-date rural institutions.

Profits from the poorer areas are drained off and concentrated in the financial centers. Yet it is these very areas which are producing the future labor supply and in which a large proportion of the prospective purchasers from industry reside. If, therefore, the opportunities of this important segment of the nation are to be more nearly equal to those of more favored groups, the financial support of rural services must be buttressed by general appropriations.

The necessity for the use of the broader tax base of the whole nation is emphasized by the increasing public welfare burdens imposed on the states. In addition to the previous heavy drain on state resources to finance education and public health, the states in the past few years have had the added responsibility of raising money for the care of all unemployables on relief and of matching the federal appropriations for the care of the aged, of the blind, and of dependent children. This extra load has made it very difficult for many of the rural states to find new sources of revenue. Clarence Heer, in a recent article,[4] pointed out that to insure the payment of very meager old-age benefits many agricultural states are expending a sixth as much as they do for education and some as much as a fifth. It is self-evident that if national standards of security and public welfare are to continue to advance, increasing participation

---

[4] "Financing the Social Security Program in the South," *Southern Economic Journal*, IV (1938), 291–302.

of the national government in equalizing state finances is necessary.

A method of equalizing rural income and at the same time of greatly enriching and strengthening rural community life is to increase the support of rural services and the number of people employed in these services in the poorer rural areas. All those organizations which go to make a balanced community life and which are taken for granted by city people are most limited in these areas, and the need for expanding these services is particularly urgent. Moreover, such an increase in the service occupations would provide uses for some of the man power no longer needed for the production of goods in agriculture and industry.

THE PROBLEM AHEAD

There is available to American agriculture sufficient good land and recoverable land to serve as a base for a sound economy. There is likewise a wealth of human resources in the farm population. There are deficiencies in techniques and in the institutional opportunities of the people and to some extent there is maladjustment through the location of too many of the people on poor land. There has also been too great disparity in the prices of farm products and the prices of commodities which farmers must buy. The favorable elements can be capitalized and the unfavorable elements do not present insuperable difficulties to a determined people. If a reasonable amount of foresight is exercised, American agriculture can be prevented from declining to the point where American farmers are forced to a peasant standard of living. However, if with the return of normal prosperity the rural sore spots are forgotten, they may be counted upon to pile up a staggering relief bill again whenever the national economy is thrown seriously out of balance.

The basic problems of rural destitution have just begun to be attacked. Although millions of rural families have received government bounties in the form of relief, the fundamental causes of rural poverty will yield only to long-time measures. The temporary return of prosperity in both agriculture and industry would have but slight effect on the hard core of rural distress and disadvantage.

Obviously some very fundamental planning is required. No program based solely on land tenure, or on tax adjustment, or on redistribution of wealth, or on any one factor whatever will meet the need. Each of these plays its part, but the human element must complement their effects in any philosophy looking toward permanently raising the level of living of the rural population.

As a nation we should be convinced that widespread need must never be permitted to occur again. The cost of constructive social programs now is a necessary price that we must pay for lack of such programs in the past. The future welfare of rural America is at stake, and inextricably bound up with the welfare of rural areas is that of the nation at large. The nation cannot be permanently prosperous unless it rests on the solid foundation of a prospering rural population.

INDEX

National Resources Board, report of, 28, 123
National Resources Committee, report of, 29
National Youth Administration:
Work projects, youth trained on, 154
Youth problems met by, 152
Negro croppers, relief grants to, average amount, 155
Negroes:
As part-time farmers, 84–85
As share tenants, 78
Negroes, rural, in industrial labor market, 64
Newell, Frederick H., 135, 136
Nonagricultural workers. *See* Relief cases, nonagricultural
Nurses, public health, in rural areas, 61

Occupational shifts, relief status and, 39–40
Occupations, definition, 83–84, 89
Osborn, Frederick, 35
Overproduction, effects of, 6

Part-time farming. *See* Farmers, part-time; Negroes; Relief cases, nonagricultural
Pellagra, 61, 125
Pioneering era, 5, 150
Population:
Age of:
Productive groups, distribution by states, 65
School groups, rural-urban distribution, 65
Excess rural, problems of, 42
Farm:
Decline in, 36–37
Migration of excess, 37
Movement of, to and from farms, 38–39, 43
Growth:
Birth rate and, 40–41
Factors in, 34
Farm as source of, 3

Industrial opportunities and, 41–42
Relief trends related to, 41
Trends in, 162, 165–166
Pressure:
Economic opportunities, maladjustment in, and, 44
In South, 124
See also Problem areas, rural
Trends, related to drought, 139
Urban:
Per cent increase in number, 37
Rural areas as source of, 3, 62–65
Working, increase in:
Future number, 43–44
Related to per capita income, 66
Poverty, rural, causes and implications of, v–vi. *See also* Rural distress
Private aid, extent of, rural-urban comparison, 10–11
Problem areas, rural:
Location of, 121
Population pressure in, 3, 37–40, 43, 44, 121, 128, 150–151
Professional groups:
Employment, productive, and, 153
Public welfare services absorbing, 153–154
Public aid, extent of:
Rural load, distribution by agencies, 156
State and local, 11
Public and private aid:
Expenditures, total, rural and town areas, 148
Number of persons receiving, 11
Purchasing power, unemployment impairing, 148

Race problems, 124
Rainfall:
In Great Plains, 134, 136, 147
In Western Cotton Area, 126–127
Land use and, 28